CHARLESTON GRILL *at* CHARLESTON PLACE

CHARLESTON GRILL *at* CHARLESTON PLACE

French-Influenced Lowcountry Cuisine

BOB WAGGONER
and
SUSAN FRANZEN

Gibbs Smith, Publisher
TO ENRICH AND INSPIRE HUMANKIND
Salt Lake City | Charleston | Santa Fe | Santa Barbara

The recipes in this book are dedicated to the memory of my mother, Barbara Ann Waggoner, who taught me how to live life to its fullest, savoring every smell and flavor. I wish the same for you.

The images in this book are dedicated to my father, Harley Waggoner, who has helped me see the world through a lens for the last twenty-five years. Without his encouragement, I would never have tackled photography late at night in my dining room at home after the restaurant had closed.

 Learning how to make smart food choices, at any age, is important for living an active, healthy life. Teaching children how to make those smart choices early is the mission of The Chef's Garden's non-profit organization, Veggie U. Helping children learn that growing, preparing and eating vegetables is not only healthy, Veggie U's 4th grade Earth to Table™ curriculum also teaches them how it can be fun. This dynamic program was implemented to promote better eating and healthy lifestyle, and it plays a part in the effort to combat the rising epidemic of childhood obesity and diabetes throughout the nation. The curriculum includes all of the materials needed to facilitate the hands-on lessons covering nutrition, agriculture, plant studies and culinary arts. This five-week, hands-on learning experience is made possible through the generous support of donors and sponsors across the United States. To learn more about this important program, please visit www.veggieu.org.

First Edition
11 10 09 08 07   5 4 3 2 1

Text © 2007 Bob Waggoner and Susan Franzen
Photographs © 2007 Bob Waggoner
www.chefbobwaggoner.com

Published by
Gibbs Smith, Publisher
P.O. Box 667
Layton, Utah 84041

Orders: 1.800.835.4993
www.gibbs-smith.com

Designed by Linda Herman
Printed and bound in China

Library of Congress Cataloging-in-Publication Data

Waggoner, Bob.
  Charleston grill at Charleston place : French-influenced lowcountry cuisine / Bob Waggoner.
     p. cm.
  ISBN-13: 978-0-941711-96-8
  ISBN-10: 0-941711-96-X
  1. Barbecue cookery. 2. Cookery, American--Southern style. I. Title.

TX840.B3W315 2007
641.7'6--dc22
                    2007017709

THANK YOUS

My mom loved the smell of roses. She always told me to take the time to stop and smell them. Roses today have no aroma. Like many of our foods, the flavor has been sacrificed to preserve it longer. You can keep roses over a week now and they smell the same as they did when you bought them . . . blah.

You can keep many foods longer than you used to, but the longer you keep them, the less flavor remains.

Not all the ingredients in my recipes are cheap or easily found. Where I can, I have suggested the best places to get the ingredients, fresh and flavorful. I believe you get what you pay for.

My recipes and ingredients are not fat free, though you may choose to substitute fat-free or low-fat ingredients. Personally, I'd rather live a short, flavorful and sweet life than a life without flavor or the smell of a rose.

I thank my wife, Christine, and daughter, Joyce, for putting up with me during this entire writing and photography madness. Joyce didn't see much of her dad this year, as it has also been the busiest year the Charleston Grill has ever had. I love them even more for sticking with me through this.

I would never have been able to pull this book off without the dedication, perseverance and friendship of Susan Franzen, my co-writer, who came up with this crazy idea in the first place.

During the writing of this book I lost my good friend, Ruth Munro, who helped me organize, type and file a lot of the recipes over the years. I miss her dearly.

My Sous Chef, Michelle Weaver, from Decatur, Alabama, has been through it all with me for thirteen years. Her hard work and drive for quality are the reasons why my restaurant is so successful and why I'm now so Southern.

A special thanks to my Sommelier, Rick Rubel, for his help with the pairings of wine with my dishes. Most of these great wine makers have become friends over the years and some are new to me, thanks to Rick's great palate.

I also thank my Charleston Grill cooks over the past ten years who have made me who I am and who created a pleasurable experience for all those who have visited the Grill. Their dedication, hard work and humor make this crazy career all worthwhile.

— Chef Bob Waggoner
Charleston Grill

CONTENTS

VEGETABLES

Collard Greens Braised in Palmetto Amber Beer   **65**

Baked Anson Mills Stone-Ground Grits with Sun-Dried Tomatoes & Fresh Goat Cheese   **66**

Roasted Corn with Smoked Bacon & Caramelized Vidalia Onions   **69**

Fennel Parmesan Gratin   **70**

Roasted Golden Beets Scented with Grand Marnier & Micro Chives   **73**

Russet Potato, Smoked Bacon & Fresh Thyme Gratin   **74**

Vegetable Pearls   **77**

Sunchokes & Haricots Verts   **78**

Grilled Okra with Maître d' Butter   **80**

Baby Turnips Braised in Port   **83**

Chanterelles, Snow Peas & Pistachios   **84**

SALADS

Soft-Shell Crab Salad   **88**

Chilled Southern Smoked Chicken, Endive & Carolina Shrimp Salad
in a Yogurt & Virgin Walnut Oil Sauce   **91**

Camembert, Marinated Grapes, Roasted Pecans & Young Arugula
in a Sherry Vinegar and Virgin Pecan Oil Dressing   **92**

Charleston Grill's Chilled Roast Duck Breast Salad with Pencil Asparagus & Poached
Button Mushrooms over Young Spinach & Duck Cracklings   **94**

Baby Lola Rosa Leaves with Clemson Blue Cheese, Marinated Shiitakes & Roasted Hazelnuts
in a Sweet Port & Fresh Rosemary Sauce   **97**

Wild Turkey Breast Salad   **98**

Sautéed Snook Salad, Elf Mushrooms in a Sherry Vinegar & Virgin Hazelnut Vinaigrette   **101**

Fried Lowcountry Oyster & White Asparagus Salad in a Chardonnay,
Anchovy & Roasted Walnut Cream   **102**

Grilled Asparagus, Smoked Salmon & Grapefruit Salad in a Citrus Pink Peppercorn Vinaigrette **105**

Warm Salmon Salad with Goat Cheese in a Tomato & Fresh Cilantro Butter **106**

Stuffed Parma Prosciutto in a Sherry Vinegar & Pecan Oil Vinaigrette **109**

Endive & Avocado Salad Scented with Lime & Pistachio Oil **110**

Sautéed Chicken Livers over Frisée in a Warm Red Wine Vinegar & Smoked Bacon Vinaigrette **113**

Veal Sweetbreads, White Asparagus & Fried Black Trumpets Salad in a Citrus Truffle Vinaigrette **114**

Bresaola, Arugula & Cèpes Salad **117**

Soups

Carolina Creek Shrimp & Lobster Bisque **120**

Charleston Grill's Yellow Tomato Gazpacho with Carolina Goat Cheese, Cucumbers & Cilantro **123**

Chilled Beet & Watermelon Soup **124**

Grilled Corn Soup with Pork Cracklings, Smoked Bacon & Thyme **127**

Roasted Garlic Soup with Parmesan & Lemon Thyme **128**

Skillet-Seared Button Mushroom Soup with Fresh Summer Truffles **131**

Green Lentil Soup with Crème Fraiche **132**

Chilled Cream of Cauliflower Scented with Nutmeg **135**

Chilled Fennel Soup with Whipped Dijon Cream & Dill **136**

He-Crab Soup **139**

Meat & Game

Carolina Quail with Country-Fried Foie Gras & Sawmill Gravy **142**

Kobe Beef Cheek Braised in Pinot Noir with Baby Carrots **144**

Seared Duck Breast in a Sherry Vinegar Lavender Honey Reduction **147**

Charleston Grill Potato Skins **148**

Pan-Seared Veal Sweetbreads in a Madeira & Sun-Dried Cherry Reduction **151**

Veal T-Bone Seared with Cèpes & Baby Carrots **152**

Pan-Seared Lamb Chops in a Niçoise Olive, Shallot & Thyme Vinaigrette   **155**

Poached and Seared Veal Tongue in a Mustard Cornichon & Fresh Tarragon Sauce   **156**

Sautéed Venison Tenderloin in a Port & Huckleberry Reduction   **159**

Baked Country Crépinette of Local Rabbit Loin, Seared Foie Gras & Vidalia Onions
in a Hollywood Sausage Sawmill Gravy   **160**

Pan-Seared Beef Tenderloin with Smoked Bacon, Button Mushrooms & Asparagus   **162**

Carolina Squab, Salsafy & Baby Vegetables in a Rosemary & Diced Liver Jus   **165**

Seared Kurabuta Pork Tenderloin in a Mustard-Chive-Dijon Cream Sauce   **166**

Roasted Chicken with Bacon & Caramelized Onions in a Jus of Seared Mushrooms   **168**

Fish

Pan-Seared Carolina Golden Trout over Young Vegetables in a Grapefruit Butter Sauce   **172**

Sautéed Barramundi over Oxtail Whipped Potatoes & Chanterelles in a Pinot Noir Butter   **174**

Jumbo Lump Blue Crab Galette in a Lime, Pear Tomato & Avocado Salsa   **177**

Spiny Lobster Baked with Fennel Butter   **178**

Grilled Atlantic Salmon with Young Fennel Bulbs in a Blood Orange Salsa   **181**

Dayboat Red Snapper Fillet over Baby Spinach, Sweet Wadmalaw Onions & Potato Pearls
in a Cinnamon Cap Mushroom Jus   **182**

Creek Flounder Sautéed in a Diced Shrimp, Lime & Caper Butter   **185**

Sautéed Carolina River Prawns with an Herbed Crème Fraiche   **186**

Frogmore Stew   **189**

Roasted Spot-Tail Bass over Green Lentils Braised in Pinot Noir   **190**

Pan-Seared Triggerfish   **192**

Grilled Spanish Mackerel with Yellow Tomatoes & Young Okra in Opal Basil Olive Vinaigrette   **195**

Black Grouper with Diver Scallop Mousse, Baked in Swiss Chard
in a Caper, Sun-Dried Tomato, Picholini Olive Butter   **196**

Okeechobee Catfish in Crayfish Sauce   **198**

DESSERTS

FOREWORD

Bob Waggoner is a Southern boy, just like me: We're both from Southern California. (Hey, if they'd drawn the Mason-Dixon Line all the way across…) I first met him back in L.A. where he was working for an innovative chef named Michael Roberts at Trumps in West Hollywood. At the time, Bob told me that he'd gotten his first culinary training when he signed up for a home economics class in high school—because he thought it would be a good place to meet girls. In other words, he had his head screwed on right even at an early age.

The next time I heard about Bob, Roberts had arranged for him to do a stage (a sort of brief, unpaid apprenticeship) with an excellent chef named Jean-Pierre Silva at his Hostellerie de Vieux Moulin, in a little village near the wine capital of Beaune in Burgundy. Lots of young Americans do stages at restaurants in France. Then they typically return to the States, luck into a job cooking at a shopping-mall restaurant named for some foodstuff or relative of the owner, and wait for Food & Wine to name them a "rising star chef" so they can get their own TV show. Not Bob. By the time he got to the Vieux Moulin, it had occurred to him that he really loved cooking and had some native talent for it—but he was also smart enough to realize that he had only just begun to learn the chef's craft.

Sensibly, he stayed on in France, and with Silva's assistance, found berths in a succession of great restaurant kitchens, some of them with three Michelin stars. The next time I saw him, he was chef de cuisine at a historic Burgundian inn, where he was not only cooking wonderful food but also speaking French so well that when he toured the dining room after lunch service to greet his customers, one after another was visibly astonished to learn that he was an American. Also in France, Bob met the one girl who mattered, a pretty French woman named Christine, whom he was wise enough to marry.

After a brief stint running his own restaurant with Christine in Burgundy, and with a detour to cook in a French restaurant in South America, Bob ended up back in his home-land, first in Nashville and then in Charleston—at Charleston Place, which he has been proud to call his professional home ever since. The rich, multi-textured, multi-cultural cui-sine of the Lowcountry, and surrounding areas of the South, gave Bob inspiration and set his imagination loose, while the incredible wealth of raw materials in the region—from grits to chicken, collards to shrimp—gave him the tools he needed to shine.

Bob is a French-trained chef in the true sense of the word—not a culinary school graduate, but a veteran of some of the best kitchens in the world, where he learned the important lessons well. Set down in a gastronomically rich part of America, he has flourished. You could call his cooking "new Southern" or Southern-French (as opposed to Southern French) if you wanted to, but it isn't really that at all: It's a cuisine based on a deep knowledge of essential technique, respect for the finest ingredients, and a sense of invention and of fun. It's Bob Waggoner cuisine. And while the average reader of this volume isn't likely to have anything approaching Bob's culinary skills or experience, he has written his recipes so logically and evocatively that you can start to make it your cuisine, too.

—Colman Andrews
Co-founder, *Saveur*
Restaurant columnist, *Gourmet*

INTRODUCTION

I remember my first job at the Sumner House steak and lobster place in the "valley." I was 17 years old and didn't know the difference between medium-rare and medium-well. No clue how the strange chef-coat thing buttoned up; it looked more like a straightjacket.

Before I knew it, my interest for cooking had developed into a passion. I collected old cookbooks as a hobby, but rarely ever opened one. That goes for trade magazines, too. We now get them by the dozen and after they've stacked up for a while I give them to my cooks.

I've never been one to copy or re-create something someone else is doing; there's not much fun in that! Unfortunately, this is the tag we have been stamped with from chefs traveling abroad and spending a week taking pictures of every dish at George Blanc when they'd be better off saving the film or disk space for the Moulin Rouge!

Anyway, these are the things I've played with over the years. Believe me, the satisfaction of your own creation being a hit is the best feeling in the world. It doesn't get any better.

I'm proud to have been a part of Charleston and the South, now well marked on the culinary map.

After thirteen years in the South I've always called my food my play on Southern traditional dishes with a French flair. People ask where dishes come from and, honestly, it is just me goofing around in the kitchen. Having great purveyors helps, too! Take a look at my favorite list on page 218. I must say that having great purveyors who are as excited about produce as you are is what really makes a chef tick—at least it works for me.

Another consideration is pairing my food with the right wine. Every dish must pass a wine test. Each wine choice listed with the recipes is from my choice producers around the world, thanks to my Sommelier, Rick Ruble. While you may not be able to find some of these specific wines in your area, stick with the winemakers and you can't go wrong.

I feel lucky to have been a part of the old school training of France; not quite the same now with the 37-hour work week.

Finding the best products is most important to the success of these dishes. Some items may cost a little more, yet I feel you get what you pay for. By the way, none of the purveyors are driving Ferraris; at least not that I know of! Great products cost more to make and ensure quality.

I can't stress enough the importance of buying from your local farmers, shrimpers and fishermen. They are out there, if you search. Find them and you'll have a better chance for flavorful ingredients that still contain important nutrients. What a concept.

Appetizers

SAMBUCA SALMON WITH AVOCADO MOUSSE
& FRIED FENNEL & LIME

1 tablespoon freshly
ground fennel seeds

BRINE

1 cup kosher salt

2/3 cup fine white sugar

SALMON

6 ounces fresh boneless,
skinless salmon

5 cranks fresh-ground
white pepper

1 shot glass Sambuca

2 tablespoons chopped
fresh tarragon leaves

1 ripe avocado, skin and
pit removed

2 limes, skin removed and
cut into segments

1 bunch chives

1 tablespoon chive blossoms

4 tablespoons fine first-press
olive oil

SERVES 2

Before grinding the fennel seeds, toast them in a small sauté pan over medium heat for approximately 1 minute to bring out the flavor.

Mix the kosher salt and white sugar for the brine and set aside.

Set the salmon in a large soup bowl and dust both sides with the ground fennel seed and fresh-ground white pepper. Drizzle the salmon with Sambuca and chopped tarragon.

Pour half the brine mixture into a glass baking dish. Remove the salmon from the soup bowl and place it in the glass dish. Pour the remaining brine mixture over the salmon. Cover with plastic wrap and refrigerate for 6 1/2 hours.

Once cured, remove the salmon from the brine mixture and gently rinse the salmon under cold water and pat dry. Wrap in plastic wrap and chill.

Slice the cured salmon as thin as you can and place flat on pre-chilled plates. Slice the avocado in 1/4-inch-thick pieces and lay with lime wedges over each slice of salmon. Garnish with chives and chive blossoms and spoon the olive oil over each salmon slice.

The salmon should be seasoned perfectly, yet you may wish to add a little fresh cracked pepper.

CHARLESTON GRILL STYLE

For a special treat, make it the way we do and add the following ingredients:

10 paper-thin slices fried fennel (1/4 fennel bulb)
1/2 cup flour
2 cups peanut or vegetable oil

Garnish with fennel sliced very thin, patted dry in a towel, tossed in flour, shaken loose and then fried quickly in peanut or vegetable oil at 350 degrees until lightly browned.

WINE PAIRING

Bruno Giacosa Roero Arneis, Piedmont 2005

YELLOWFIN TUNA CARPACCIO IN A PASSION
FRUIT, LIME & FRESH MINT VINAIGRETTE

2 slices country French bread

1/4 cup olive oil to drizzle

1 small head frisée

1 pound (4 ounces per person) highest quality grade raw tuna, sliced 1/4 inch thick

Edible orchid flower petals (optional)

1 bunch chive tips, cut

VINAIGRETTE

8 small passion fruits (equals 1/2 cup passion fruit juice)

1/2 lime, juiced

1/2 teaspoon kosher salt

4 cranks fresh-ground white pepper

2 shallots, peeled and chopped fine

8 mint leaves, sliced fine at the last minute

1 tablespoon pink peppercorns

3 tablespoons olive oil

SERVES 4

Preheat oven to 350 degrees.

Slice the bread lengthwise into 1/2-inch strips, drizzle with olive oil and bake until toasted or, even better, grill on the barbecue. Keep warm in the oven until serving.

Remove the bottoms of the frisée and rinse in cold water. Dry gently in a towel.

Prepare the vinaigrette by slicing the passion fruit in half. Strain the juice and discard the seeds. Add the lime juice, salt, white pepper and shallots.

Place the tuna in the center of a chilled plate.

Just before serving, gently mix the sliced mint, pink peppercorns and olive oil to the passion fruit mix. Drizzle the vinaigrette over and around the tuna. Garnish with orchid flower petals, grilled breadsticks, chive tips and frisée.

Serve this dish very cold with very cold plates. You can prepare this an hour ahead of time by putting the sliced tuna on a plate covered with plastic wrap. Press down on the plastic wrap to protect the tuna from any air. Store this in your refrigerator until ready to serve.

WINE PAIRING

Greenhough Sauvignon Blanc, Nelson 2005

PAN-SEARED DIVER SCALLOPS
IN AN ORANGE-SAFFRON SAUCE

12 large (dry-pack)
   diver scallops

2 tablespoons kosher salt,
   divided

7 cranks fresh-ground
   white pepper, divided

1 tablespoon unsalted butter

2 shallots, chopped fine

2 oranges, juiced

1 teaspoon saffron pistils
   steeped in 2 tablespoons
   hot water

3 tablespoons unsalted butter,
   cut into cubes and chilled

1 bunch fresh chervil

1 bunch chives

SERVES 4

Season all sides of the scallops with 1 1/2 tablespoons salt and 5 cranks of pepper.

Heat 1 tablespoon of butter in a medium-sized pan. Once melted, add 6 scallops and sear over medium-high heat without shaking. If they stick to the pan, that's more flavor for the sauce later.

Sear the scallops for 20 seconds on each side until brown. Repeat for the remaining 6 scallops.

Remove the scallops and return the pan to the heat. Add the chopped shallots to the pan and gently cook 20 seconds without browning. Add the orange juice and saffron water, and reduce to a thick syrup consistency over medium heat.

Lower the heat and whisk in the chilled butter. Add 1 teaspoon salt and 2 cranks of pepper if needed.

Place 3 scallops per person in a small soup bowl. Gently spoon the saffron, orange, and butter mixture over the scallops and garnish with chervil and chives.

If you're worried about whether the scallops are cooked or not, under-cooked scallops are tons better than overcooked ones.

Ask for dry-pack scallops from the fish market, as you probably won't find these in the grocery store.

WINE PAIRING

Château Smith-Haut-Lafitte, Pessac-Léognan 2003

ZUCCHINI BLOSSOMS STUFFED WITH CAROLINA SHRIMP MOUSSE

CAROLINA SHRIMP MOUSSE

14 ounces fresh wild American shrimp, peeled and deveined (I prefer Carolina shrimp)

1 1/2 cups heavy whipping cream

1 tablespoon kosher salt

4 cranks fresh-ground white pepper

8 young female zucchini with blossoms attached (ask for these at your farmers market)

4 tablespoons butter at room temperature

SAUCE

1 cup Noilly Prat (dry French vermouth)

1 cup dry white wine (Sauvignon Blanc or Chardonnay)

2 shallots, chopped fine

8 tablespoons cold butter, diced

24 currant tomatoes

1 tablespoon chopped opal basil

1 tablespoon capers

1 teaspoon kosher salt or to taste

2 to 3 cranks fresh-ground white pepper or to taste

NOTE: Shrimp now has to carry a label with the country of origin. U.S. shrimp are the best.

SERVES 4

Purée the shrimp in a food processor. Slowly blend in the heavy cream to thicken (about 20 seconds). Then season with salt and pepper. Do not over purée or the mix will heat up.

TIP: Place your empty food processor bowl and blade in the freezer an hour before blending the shrimp mix.

Fill a pastry bag with the shrimp mousse and fill the zucchini flowers 3/4 full with the mousse. The easiest way I've found is to hold the blossom like you're holding an ice cream cone. With a forceful blow into the flower, it will open. Insert the tip of the pastry bag into the open flower and gently squeeze. Twist the ends of the flower to hold the mousse. Place the zucchini blossoms on a lightly buttered baking sheet and brush each blossom with the butter to keep them from drying out.

In a small saucepan over medium heat, reduce the Noilly Prat and wine with shallots to 1/4 cup. Reduce the heat to low and stir the butter in slowly. Add the tomatoes, basil and capers.

Do not season until you have tasted the sauce with the capers so you'll know how much salt they have given to the sauce.

Salt to taste and add 2 to 3 cranks of pepper.

Preheat oven to 375 degrees.

Bake the blossoms for 4 to 5 minutes. They are cooked when firm to the touch. Remove from oven and place on individual plates. Immediately spoon the sauce over the blossoms and serve. They're at their best right out of the oven. Each plate should have six of the currant tomatoes.

You may also serve this as a vegetable to accompany your favorite fish. And, if you don't have a dinner budget, try replacing the shrimp with lobster.

If this recipe doesn't accomplish anything else, it will at least get you out talking to your local farmer while looking for the zucchini blossoms. He needs your help and you need to eat more vegetables!

WINE PAIRING

J.M. Boillot Rully Mont Palais, 1er Cru, Burgundy 2004

CHARLESTON GRILL OYSTER SHOOTER

1/4 cup Sauvignon Blanc

1 small shallot, chopped fine

1 tablespoon unsalted
butter, chilled

2 cranks fresh-ground
white pepper

1/4 teaspoon salt

Zest of 1/2 lime, chopped
fine or grated

4 fresh shucked oysters (save
the juice from the shells)

4 small shot glasses

1 tablespoon finely diced
cucumber, skin on

1 sprig chervil, picked
leaves only

SERVES 4

Heat the wine and shallot in a small saucepan over medium heat, reducing by half. Reduce the heat to low and whisk in butter, pepper, salt and lime zest. Remove from heat and keep warm (if the sauce cools it will break; do not re-boil).

Gently drop 1 oyster into each of the shot glasses. Add 1/4 of the diced cucumber and some chervil leaves.

Just before serving, add the oyster juice to the warm sauce and spoon just enough into each shot glass to cover the oyster, then down that puppy! Chin-Chin.

Remember, like any other shot, it's all got to fit in your mouth, so don't over-fill the shot glasses. Yes, the oyster is raw; just try it!

WINE PAIRING

Beer: Ayinger Oktober Fest-Märzen

GRILLED DIVER SCALLOPS WITH A PINEAPPLE, CILANTRO & PINK PEPPERCORN SALSA

SALSA

1/2 ripe, fresh pineapple, diced fine

1 tablespoon pink pepper-corns

1 tablespoon coriander seeds

3 limes, juiced

2 teaspoons kosher salt

5 cranks fresh-ground white pepper

2 shallots, chopped fine

6 tablespoons virgin olive oil

1/2 bunch fresh cilantro (leaves only), chopped at the last minute

SCALLOPS

2 tablespoons kosher salt

8 cranks fresh-ground white pepper

16 large diver scallops

Olive oil

SERVES 4

You may want to make the salsa the day before serving and just add the oil and fresh cilantro at the last minute.

Finely dice the pineapple and mix together with the pink peppercorns, coriander seeds, lime juice, salt and pepper. Add the raw shallots, olive oil and fresh chopped cilantro.

Keep the salsa as cold as possible. The fun of this dish is the hot-cold, sweet-acid sensation.

For the scallops, sprinkle the salt and pepper over all sides of the scallops and cover all sides with a small amount of olive oil.

On a very hot grill, cook the scallops 30 seconds on each side, keeping the grill top open. Overcooked scallops are terrible, so you'll want to keep them a nice medium-rare. Remove the scallops from the grill and arrange 4 scallops on each plate. Cover each scallop with 1/2 tablespoon of the pineapple salsa and serve.

TIP: Lesser-quality scallops are soaking in juice—if these are the only ones available, let them dry on a towel several minutes ahead of time. Better yet, save this recipe until you find great diver scallops!

TIP: To retain the color of the herb when chopping herbs like cilantro, use the sharpest knife in the kitchen rather than pinching it with a dull knife.

If you're lucky enough to live in an area where you can purchase scallops in the shell, use the half-shell as your plate. Best of all, you will know the scallops are fresh.

WINE PAIRING

Glatzer Grüner Veltliner, Carnuntum 2004

SEARED DUCK FOIE GRAS OVER HUSHPUPPIES
STUFFED WITH FIGS

POMEGRANATE WHIPPED CREAM

4 ounces fresh heavy cream, chilled

1 teaspoon salt

2 cranks fresh-ground white pepper

1 tablespoon pomegranate molasses (Cortas brand; product of Lebanon)

1/2 tablespoon pomegranate molasses for garnish

HUSHPUPPIES

6 cups oil (enough to cover the batter)

3 cups cornmeal

1 cup cake flour

1 teaspoon baking powder

1 whole egg

1 Vidalia onion, diced fine

1 1/2 teaspoons kosher salt

4 cranks fresh-ground white pepper

2 1/2 cups buttermilk

FIG COMPOTE

1 1/2 pounds fresh mission figs

4 tablespoons unsalted butter

1/2 cup wild clover honey

1 teaspoon salt

3 cranks fresh-ground white pepper

MAIN DISH

4 Hushpuppy Shells, hollowed out, insides discarded

4 (4-ounce) thick slices duck foie gras

SERVES 4

Make the Pomegranate Whipped Cream first as it will need to chill while you prepare the rest of this dish. Chilling the mixing bowl in advance helps the cream whip best.

In a cold mixing bowl, whip the fresh heavy cream. Do not over beat. Add salt and pepper and fold in 1 tablespoon of molasses gently with a rubber spatula or whisk. Refrigerate.

Preheat oven to 300 degrees.

To make the hushpuppy shells, begin by heating the oil to 350 degrees in a deep pot.

In a large bowl, mix the rest of the hushpuppy ingredients, adding the buttermilk last, to form a stiff batter. With two large kitchen spoons, form the batter into 2 egg-shaped balls. You will be making a shell, not a true hushpuppy.

Gently drop the batter into the hot oil and fry until golden brown. The oil should cover the batter. Once the batter is golden brown, carefully remove it from the oil and place on a baking sheet. Bake for 5 to 10 minutes or until the batter is dry.

Let the hushpuppies rest for 45 minutes. After they have rested, carefully slice each hushpuppy in half lengthwise with a serrated knife. Gently scoop out the insides to form a bowl shape. Keep at room temperature.

Prepare the compote by trimming the stems from the tops of the figs. Quarter the figs. Melt the butter in a large pan over medium-high heat until light brown. Add the figs and cook, stirring constantly until figs are syrupy, 20 to 25 minutes. If you can get a light sear on them they will have a better flavor.

Add honey, salt and pepper to taste and remove from heat. Let figs rest approximately 10 minutes in pan, allowing them to absorb the honey.

Fill the hushpuppy shells with 2 ounces (approximately 2 tablespoons) of the Fig Compote and place in oven until hot, approximately 5 minutes.

Season both sides of the foie gras with salt and pepper and then place gently in a very hot and dry sauté pan. Cast iron works best.

To keep your smoke alarm from going off, open a window in your kitchen or turn on your exhaust fan before searing the foie gras. Sear both sides of the foie gras, 10 to 15 seconds each until golden brown. Place the foie gras in the oven until it springs to the touch, approximately 3 minutes.

Place a small amount of the compote in the center of the each plate and cement a stuffed hushpuppy on top of the compote.

Remove the foie gras from the pan gently, using a spatula to remove it from its own juices. Carefully place it, prettiest side up, on top of the hushpuppy.

Place a small pinch of sprouts or chives on top of the foie gras.

Place 2 teaspoons Pomegranate Whipped Cream on top of the sprouts. Sprinkle a few pomegranate seeds (if you can find them) on top of the pomegranate cream and finish off with a few more sprouts, chive tips and edible flowers.

Drizzle the reserved molasses gently over the foie gras (approximately 1 tablespoon per person).

WINE PAIRING
Qupé Syrah, Central Coast 2003

1 teaspoon salt

4 cranks fresh white ground pepper

Sprouts or chives

1/2 pomegranate, seeded

Edible flowers (optional)

FLORIDA STONE CRAB CLAWS WITH A DIJON MUSTARD & FRESH TARRAGON CRÈME FRAICHE

12 medium-sized stone crab claws (see purveyors' page for where we get them)

1/2 cup crème fraiche (you can substitute sour cream)

1 large lime, juiced

1 teaspoon kosher salt

3 cranks fresh-ground white pepper

2 teaspoons Dijon mustard

1 tablespoon chopped fresh tarragon

Chive tips for garnish

Tarragon sprouts for garnish

SERVES 2

Whack the stone crab claws with a wooden mallet or the backside of a heavy chef's knife. They should split easily without damaging the pincer shell. Remove the elbow meat and set aside.

Remove the shell from the claw, leaving the pincher shell attached. You'll use the pincher to dip the claw into the sauce and keep your fingers clean.

In a small bowl, gently whisk the crème fraiche (or sour cream) and add the lime juice, salt and pepper. Add the mustard, the tarragon and elbow crab meat; then chill for at least 30 minutes. It's best when cold!

When you're ready to serve, make a small mound of the elbow crabmeat sauce in the center of a pretty bowl. Arrange the crab claws around the mound, garnish with chive tips and tarragon sprouts. Serve cold and enjoy by dipping the claws into the sauce.

Thanks to Florida State Law, the great part of this dish is that there's no cooking involved. The claws always come freshly steamed off the boat!

This is a fun appetizer for a picnic or get together; everyone has fun with it.

WINE PAIRING

Iron Horse Russian Cuvée, Sonoma-Green Valley 2000

WARM GOAT CHEESE & GOLDEN BEET TART
IN A GARDEN KUMQUAT VINAIGRETTE

SERVES 2

TART

6 baby golden beets, unpeeled

1 cup vegetable oil

1 large sheet puff pastry

1 tablespoon virgin olive oil, divided

1 shallot, chopped fine

1/4 cup whipping cream

6 ounces fresh goat cheese

1 tablespoon salt

3 cranks fresh-ground white pepper

VINAIGRETTE

2 limes, juiced

1 tablespoon salt

2 cranks fresh-ground white pepper

2 small, fresh kumquats

1 tablespoon micro chives or chive tips

3 tablespoons virgin olive oil

Preheat oven to 325 degrees.

Rinse the beets under cold running water, place in a large bowl, pour 1 cup of oil over them and roll them in your hands to cover each with oil. Next, transfer them to a roasting pan with 2 1/2 cups water, and cover with aluminum foil. Bake for 1 1/2 hours until tender. Remove and let cool.

Once cool to the touch, squeeze the beets to remove the skins; discard skins. Cut the beets in half and set aside.

Preheat oven to 350 degrees.

Lay the puff pastry over two 2-inch tart shell pans and poke holes in the dough. If possible, place another pan on top of the pastry to fit snug and to prevent the dough from puffing. Bake at 350 degrees for 15-20 minutes, checking often. Press the dough down as it bakes. You'll want a thin, flaky dough, not puffed. Once cooked, remove the top pan. Remove the tart shell and bake the pastry on its own another couple of minutes to create a dry and flaky shell.

In a small saucepan, heat 1/2 tablespoon olive oil and gently cook the chopped shallot, without browning, for 1 1/2 minutes over low heat.

Add the whipping cream and bring it to a gentle boil. Add the goat cheese, salt and pepper.

Gently press the goat cheese with a wooden spoon to make a paste as it heats. Do not cook long as this is only to warm the cheese and season it.

Once warm, spoon the cheese evenly and gently into the baked tart shells. Arrange the baby beets halves thinly on top of the warm goat cheese mix.

Place the filled tart shells on a baking sheet and bake at 325 degrees for 4 minutes.

To make the vinaigrette, juice the two limes and add salt and pepper. Remove the seeds from the kumquats and slice; add the slices to the lime

juice. Add the chives and 3 tablespoons olive oil.

Remove the tart shells from the oven and place in the center of the plate, spooning the vinaigrette over the beets, ensuring that each gets some kumquat slices. Dipping the spoon to the bottom of the vinaigrette will get the full vinaigrette flavor.

TIP: You can make the tart shells in advance as long as you keep them in an airtight container. Make extras because some may break.

WINE PAIRING
Brocard Chablis Forchaume, 1er Cru, Burgundy 2004

PAN-SEARED VEAL SWEETBREADS WITH ROASTED GARLIC IN A JUS DE VIANDE WITH WILD CHANTERELLES OVER CAROLINA STONE-GROUND GRITS

GRITS

2 cups chicken stock

2 tablespoons Plugra brand unsalted butter

1/2 cup stone-ground whole grain grits

2 cups heavy cream, divided

1 teaspoon salt

4 to 6 cranks fresh-ground white pepper

12 cloves garlic, tossed in 1 tablespoon olive oil and baked for 1 hour at 275 degrees until soft

VEAL SWEETBREADS

4 (about 1 1/2 pounds) fresh veal sweetbreads (remove the fatty membrane with a paring knife)

4 teaspoons salt

16 cranks fresh-ground white pepper

2 tablespoons vegetable oil or grapeseed oil

2 tablespoons whole butter, divided

8 tablespoons fresh shallots, chopped fine

12 chanterelles, cleaned and split in half

1 1/2 tablespoons kosher salt

3 cranks white pepper

1 cup Chardonnay

3 cups rich veal stock

1 bunch fresh chives

To prepare the grits, heat the chicken stock and butter together in a heavy-bottomed saucepan and bring to a boil. Stir in the grits and return the mixture to a boil.

Reduce heat allowing the grits to simmer for 12 minutes, stirring occasionally to prevent them from sticking.

Add 1/2 cup cream to the pot and turn down the heat, allowing the grits to simmer for another 10 minutes.

As the liquid is absorbed, add the rest of the cream as needed with a total cooking time of about 1 1/2 hours. No quick grits in the South!

Add salt and pepper along with the roasted garlic.

The grits should have a lightly soupy look to them, but not enough to run on the plate.

After cleaning the sweetbreads, run cold water over them for 15 minutes to remove any blood. Dry them on paper towels. Sprinkle 1/2 teaspoon salt and 2 cranks pepper on each side of each sweetbread.

Heat the oil in a large skillet on high heat. When it is hot, add 1 tablespoon butter and add the sweetbreads one at a time, but quickly. Do not shake the pan or move the sweetbreads once you have placed them in the pan. If they stick to the bottom of the pan, that's more flavor for your sauce.

Cook the sweetbreads 2 1/2 minutes on each side to a light golden brown color. Remove the browned sweetbreads from the pan and eliminate the excess oil.

In the same pan, add remaining butter along with shallots and cook over low heat for 1 minute. You'll want them a golden brown as well. If they burn at all your sauce will be bitter.

Toss the chanterelles in the pan and gently turn them over (you may need to add a little more butter if they're too dry). Sauté with 1 1/2 tablespoons

kosher salt and 3 cranks of pepper and cook for another 2 minutes. Remove the chanterelles from the pan. Chanterelles are best when tossed in hot butter and cooked al dente; if browned they become bitter.

Deglaze the pan with the wine; reduce by half. Add the veal stock and reduce to a sauce consistency. Add the chives, sweetbreads and chanterelles back into the sauce and spoon over the grits.

WINE PAIRING
Latour Bienvenues-Bâtard-Montrachet Grand Cru 1997

PAN-SEARED FOIE GRAS OVER
CARAMELIZED GRANNY SMITH APPLES

1/4 cup boiling hot water

1 ounce French cognac

1/2 cup dried golden raisins

1/4 cup whipping cream (no sugar added)

1 tablespoon 100% pure maple syrup

1 Granny Smith apple

1 tablespoon butter

1 tablespoon sugar

1 teaspoon salt

4 cranks fresh-ground white pepper

6 ounces fresh, grade-A foie gras lobe

3 tablespoons pecans tossed in honey and baked at 350 degrees for 5 minutes

Fresh chives or sprouts for garnish

SERVES 2

Pour the hot water and cognac over the raisins and cover to plump for about 20 minutes.

Whip the cream semi-stiff with a touch of salt and pepper. Gently fold in the maple syrup and refrigerate.

Peel and core the apple and cut into 8 wedges. Heat the butter in a small sauté pan over medium-high heat. Add the apple wedges and sprinkle sugar over them.

Caramelize the apples on each side for about 1 1/2 minutes each. When the apples have browned, strain the raisins and add them to the pan to produce a small amount of juice. Set aside and keep warm.

Heat a dry iron skillet until it's almost smoking. Salt and pepper the foie gras slices and sear them in the pan until browned, about 1 minute each side (you may need to turn the heat down).

Spoon the apples, raisins and juice into a bowl. Lay the seared foie gras on top and spoon 1 tablespoon whipped maple cream on top of the foie gras. Sprinkle the pecans, chives, or sprouts on top of the foie gras to garnish.

WINE PAIRING

Arrowood Riesling Special Select, Late Harvest, California 1997

POACHED EGGS IN PINOT NOIR WITH YOUNG ZUCCHINI BLOSSOMS STUFFED WITH PULLED PIG'S FEET "FAĆON BOURGUIGNON"

STUFfiNG

1 cup vegetable oil

2 fresh pig's feet trotters, split in half

3 tablespoons unsalted butter

1 large carrot, peeled and diced

1 large onion, peeled and diced

3 cloves garlic, split in half

3 branches fresh thyme

2 branches fresh rosemary

2 bay leaves

6 juniper berries

6 white peppercorns

1 small leek, split, washed and diced

1 teaspoon salt

5 cranks fresh-ground white pepper

2 bottles Pinot Noir (save 2 cups to poach eggs)

1 Vidalia onion, sliced and caramelized

2 teaspoons salt

3 cranks white pepper

12 fresh zucchini blossoms

1/2 cup veal stock

SAUCE

2 tablespoons diced, smoked bacon

24 small pearl onions, peeled

24 small button mushrooms, cleaned and cut in half

1 tablespoon chopped fresh flat-leaf parsley

4 fresh large eggs

Young parsley sprouts

SERVES 4

Preheat oven to 300 degrees.

In a large pot, heat 1 cup vegetable oil over medium heat. Brown the pig's feet for 5 minutes on each side; do not blacken. Discard the oil from the pot and set the pig's feet aside.

In the same pot, heat 3 tablespoons unsalted butter and cook the remaining stuffing ingredients (except the wine, onion, salt, pepper, zucchini blossoms and veal stock) over medium heat until lightly browned. Add red wine and bring to a boil.

Add the seared pig's feet to the pot of red wine and submerge them completely. Cover the pot and bake for 3 hours. Remove the pig's feet from the pot. Once the pig's feet reach room temperature, pull the meat from the bones. Discard the bones. Save the liquid in the pot.

Dice the meat and add the caramelized onion. Add the salt and 3 cranks of pepper.

Stuff the zucchini blossoms with the onion and meat mixture. Brush the flower with melted butter so it doesn't dry out, then set aside on a buttered baking sheet.

Pass the red wine/pig's feet cooking liquid through a strainer and cook the strained liquid over low heat until reduced to 1 cup of liquid. Add the veal stock and bring to a simmer. Set aside the sauce. Salt and pepper to taste (approximately 1/2 teaspoon salt and 2 cranks pepper).

In a small Teflon pan, sear the smoked bacon and add the pearl onions and button mushrooms until lightly brown. Add salt sparingly (because of the bacon) and fresh-ground white pepper. Add the chopped parsley, bacon mushrooms and pearl onions to the red wine–veal stock reduction, and reduce to a sauce consistency.

To prepare the eggs, heat 2 cups of red wine to simmering in a small pot. Drop the eggs in to poach for approximately 2 to 2 1/2 minutes.

Bake the zucchini blossoms at 400 degrees for 3 to 5 minutes.

Place the poached eggs in a bowl with the zucchini blossoms alongside and spoon the red wine, mushroom, bacon and onion sauce over them. Garnish with young parsley sprouts.

WINE PAIRING

J.L. Chave St.-Joseph Offerus, Rhône Valley 2003

ESCARGOT

1/2 pound unsalted butter, at room temperature

1 small shallot, chopped fine

2 teaspoons finely chopped garlic

3 heaping teaspoons chervil, leaves picked

5 heaping teaspoons parsley, leaves picked only

2 teaspoons cognac

4 teaspoons white wine (Chardonnay or Sauvignon Blanc)

1 1/2 teaspoons salt

1 1/2 teaspoons fresh-ground white pepper

SNAILS

24 snail shells

24 canned snails

Sliced country French bread

SERVES 4

To make the butter, mix all ingredients together in a mixer. If you make this the day before, wrap well before placing in your refrigerator so the garlic odor doesn't spread.

Place 1/2 teaspoon of maitre d' butter into each snail shell and then drop 1 snail on top of the butter. Completely cover each snail with the rest of the butter.

Cover a baking sheet with kosher salt and place the snails on top of the salt so they don't tip over during cooking. Bake at 375 degrees for 5 to 7 minutes until hot and the butter is melted. Cut the French bread into finger-sized pieces. Serve the fingers of crusty bread to dip into the shells for the lovely leftover butter.

WINE PAIRING

Au Bon Climat Pinot Noir Sanford and Benedict Vineyard, Santa Ynez Valley 2005

CHARLESTON GRILL LOBSTER TEMPURA
WITH CREAMY STONE-GROUND GRITS

GRITS

2 cups chicken stock

2 1/2 tablespoons unsalted butter

1/2 cup stone-ground grits

1 to 2 cups heavy cream, divided

1 teaspoon salt

4 to 6 cranks fresh-ground white pepper

1 teaspoon fresh lemon zest, chopped fine

SAUCE

2 cups Chardonnay

1/2 cup Noilly Prat vermouth

3 shallots, chopped fine

8 tablespoons unsalted butter, diced

1 teaspoon salt

3 cranks fresh-ground white pepper

2 tablespoons fresh tarragon leaves

1 large yellow tomato, peeled, seeded and diced

LOBSTER TEMPURA

1/4 teaspoon salt per tail

1 crank fresh-ground white pepper per tail

4 small fresh lobster tails, pre-steamed 5 minutes each, meat removed from shells

1 cup all-purpose flour

1 cup heavy cream

1 medium-sized green tomato, peeled, seeded and cut into cubes

SERVES 4

For the grits, bring the chicken stock and butter to a boil in a thick-bottomed saucepan. Stir in the grits and return to a boil. Reduce the heat, allowing the grits to cook for another 5 minutes at a simmer until the grits are thick and have absorbed most of the chicken stock. Stir occasionally to keep the grits from sticking.

Add 1/2 cup of the heavy cream to the pot and reduce the heat allowing the grits to cook slowly for another 10 minutes. As the liquid is absorbed, add more cream, cooking the grits until the desired consistency. Add the salt and pepper.

With a total cooking time of at least an hour, the grits should be thick and full-bodied. Fold in the lemon zest just before serving. Spoon 2 tablespoons of grits into a soup bowl.

To prepare the sauce, heat the wine, vermouth and shallots together in a small saucepan. Reduce to 3 tablespoons. With a small whip, add the butter cubes a little at a time over low heat. Whip slowly to emulsify the butter. Add salt and pepper. Just before serving, add the fresh tarragon and yellow tomato. Spoon 1 tablespoon of the sauce over the grits.

For the lobster tempura, salt and pepper each tail and cut them in half, lengthwise. Toss each tail in the flour, then the heavy cream, then back into the flour. Drop the lobster tails and green tomato into a small deep fryer at 375 degrees for approximately 1 minute until brown. Gently set the lobster tempura and fried tomatoes on top of the grits.

This is a great appetizer. Don't overcook the lobster, just make it crispy quickly.

WINE PAIRING

Soligo Prosecco Brut, Veneto

BREAKFAST

PAIN PERDU

1 cup whole milk

2 large eggs, gently beaten

2 1/2-inch-thick slices
country French bread (select
the French bread that looks
like half a basketball; the
drier the better!)

6 tablespoons white sugar

2 tablespoons unsalted butter

SERVES 2

Pour the milk into a Pyrex dish (or another glass dish large enough to hold the bread and milk).

Pour the eggs into a separate Pyrex dish.

Set the bread slices on top of the milk in the first Pyrex dish and let them soak for about 1 minute each side.

Gently transfer the bread slices to the Pyrex dish with the eggs. Let the bread soak for about 30 seconds each side and remove them, letting the excess egg drip off.

Place the bread slices on a large plate and sprinkle the top of each slice with approximately 1 1/2 tablespoons sugar (enough to cover the top).

Heat the butter over medium heat in a large Teflon pan. Place the bread slices, sugar side down into the hot butter and cook until brown. The sugar will caramelize on the bread after about 2 to 3 minutes; check often.

While the sugar side is browning, sprinkle the remaining sugar on top of the bread slices. Turn the bread slices over with a large plastic spatula and brown the other side for 2 to 3 minutes. Keep finished slices warm in a hot oven and serve all at once.

The sugar in this recipe replaces our maple syrup, but I still love true maple syrup on this true French toast.

GAUFFRES

1 split vanilla bean, scraped into 2 cups whole milk

2 cups all-purpose flour

1 teaspoon salt

2 teaspoons baking powder

2 egg whites

4 teaspoons sugar

2 egg yolks

2 tablespoons vegetable oil

SERVES 6-8

Cook vanilla bean in milk. Bring to a boil and simmer 2 minutes, then chill.

In a bowl, mix the flour, salt and baking powder together. Set aside.

Whip the egg whites and then slowly add the sugar to create stiff peaks.

Remove the vanilla-milk mixture from the refrigerator and add the egg yolks to this mixture. Remove the vanilla bean and pour the milk mixture into the flour mix, whisking to a smooth batter (no lumps).

Add the vegetable oil to the batter. Gently whisk in half of the whipped egg whites, then fold in the remaining egg whites.

Oil your waffle iron and heat it. Add enough batter to just cover the iron. Cook 2 to 3 minutes and serve with Bliss maple syrup.

Preheating your waffle iron is a big bonus when making waffles.

CRÊPES

2 cups flour

1 teaspoon sugar

1 pinch salt

2 eggs, beaten

1 2/3 cups milk

1/3 cup water

1 tablespoon melted butter

1 tablespoon orange zest

1 tablespoon lemon zest

2 tablespoons Grand Marnier

Nutella, preserves, honey or
   plain white sugar

MAKES 6 CRÊPES

Sift the flour, sugar and salt into a bowl and make a well in the center. Mix the eggs and milk with the water, and pour slowly into the well, whisking all the time to incorporate the flour mixture until you have a smooth batter. Add the melted butter and cover. Let rest for at least 1 hour.

Just before making the crêpes, add the orange and lemon zest, as well as the Grand Marnier.

Heat a crêpe pan or nonstick saucepan and grease with a small amount of melted butter. Pour in enough batter to barely cover the bottom of the pan and quickly lean the pan sideways to spread the batter as thin as you can across the bottom of the pan. Cook for 20 seconds until lightly brown.

Flip the crêpe and cook for 20 seconds on the other side. Serve with Nutella, preserves or honey and plain sugar.

My daughter, Joyce, would live on crêpes and Nutella if I'd let her. (Nutella is a sweet, hazelnut chocolate spread found in most high-end supermarkets.)

I always think of champagne with crêpes. Champagne isn't the best with chocolate, but it's another reason to drink champagne!

SHRIMP & GRITS, CHARLESTON GRILL STYLE

GRITS

2 1/4 cups chicken stock

2 1/2 tablespoons unsalted butter

1/2 cup stone-ground grits (we use Anson Mills)

1 to 2 cups heavy cream, divided

1 tablespoon salt or to taste

4 cranks fresh-cracked white pepper

1 teaspoon fresh lemon zest, chopped fine

SHRIMP

8 wild American shrimp, peeled and deveined

1 tablespoon salt

4 to 5 cranks fresh-ground white pepper

2 tablespoons olive oil, divided

1 teaspoon finely chopped garlic

2 teaspoons chopped shallots

1 yellow tomato, peeled, seeded and diced

1/2 cup dry white wine

1/4 cup heavy cream

1 tablespoon finely chopped opal basil

Chives or sprouts for garnish

SERVES 2

Preparing grits takes about 1 hour minimum total cooking time. Bring the chicken stock and butter to a boil in a thick-bottomed saucepan. Stir in the grits and return to a boil.

Reduce the heat, allowing the grits to cook for another 15 minutes at a low boil until the grits are thick and have absorbed most of the chicken stock. Stir often to keep the grits from sticking.

Add 1/2 cup of the heavy cream to the pot and reduce the heat, allowing the grits to cook slowly for another 10 minutes.

As the liquid is absorbed, add more cream, cooking the grits until thick and full bodied. Add salt and pepper to taste. Fold in the lemon zest just before serving.

To prepare the shrimp, salt and pepper the shrimp on each side. In a large pan, heat 1 tablespoon oil until almost smoking hot, then add the shrimp. Cook the shrimp for 15 seconds on each side and remove from the pan. The shrimp will still be raw in the center.

Remove the oil from the pan and discard. In the same pan, add the remaining oil over low heat.

Add the garlic and shallots to the pan and cook for 30 seconds. Add the tomato and white wine. When the wine is reduced by half, add the cream and reduce to a sauce consistency. Taste to see if more salt or pepper is needed.

Place the shrimp in the hot sauce and add the basil. Turn off the heat. Let the shrimp sit in the hot sauce for 30 seconds to finish cooking.

Spoon 4 shrimp per person over the grits with some sauce. Garnish with chives or sprouts.

TIP: You can burn the skin off the tomato on an open flame and chill under ice water for easy skin removal; you may also blanch the tomato in boiling water and then chill to remove the skin or use pear tomatoes as shown in the photo.

HERB OMELET

5 tablespoons butter, divided

2 shallots, chopped fine

1 clove garlic, chopped fine

2 1/2 tablespoons chopped parsley

2 1/2 tablespoons chopped basil

1 tablespoon chopped tarragon

10 eggs

2 1/2 tablespoons heavy cream

1 1/2 tablespoons salt

6 cranks cracked pepper

SERVES 4

In a small sauté pan, heat 1 tablespoon butter and gently cook the shallots and garlic without browning, just sweat them. Add the parsley, basil and tarragon and cook 10 seconds. Remove from heat.

Mix the eggs and cream together with the salt and pepper. Whisk to break the eggs. Add the herb/shallot mix to the eggs and whisk.

Heat 1 tablespoon butter in a nonstick fry pan over medium heat and add 1/4 of the egg mix. Stir often as though you're making scrambled eggs. As the mixture pulls together, drop the heat. Lift the handle of the pan and, at the same time, use a spatula to help the eggs fall to the bottom of the pan. Fold the omelet onto a plate. Repeat for the remaining 3/4 of the egg mix.

Other herbs, like thyme, chives and rosemary, also work well.

TIP: When cooking an omelet, if the eggs cook together enough to fold you're fine. Don't think you need to cook it another 7 minutes to be safe.

SCRAMBLED EGGS WITH SEARED PORTOBELLO MUSHROOMS, SMOKED BACON & GRUYERE CHEESE

3 slices smoked bacon, cut into small pieces

1 small onion, sliced fine

2 medium-sized portobello mushrooms, stems and gills removed

1 teaspoon salt

3 cranks fresh-ground white pepper

6 large fresh eggs, whipped lightly

3 tablespoons shaved Gruyere cheese

1 teaspoon fresh thyme

2 slices country French bread

SERVES 2

In a medium-sized Teflon pan, cook the bacon pieces over medium heat until lightly browned. Remove the bacon and set aside.

Add the onion to the bacon fat and lightly brown for 1 minute. Add the mushrooms and cook for another 30 seconds. Salt and pepper lightly.

Add the bacon back to the pan and fold in the whipped eggs. Season with remaining salt and pepper, being careful not to add too much salt as the bacon and the Gruyere will add salt to the dish.

Cook the eggs to your own preference; the French like them somewhat runny. Just before serving, add the Gruyere cheese and thyme.

Serve hot over a slice of toasted country French bread.

I enjoy this with French gherkins and Dijon mustard on the side.

SCRAMBLED EGGS IN THE SHELL WITH TRUFFLES

6 whole eggs

1 tablespoon unsalted butter

2 shallots, chopped fine

1/2 tablespoon salt

4 cranks fresh-ground
white pepper

1 ounce truffles, sliced thin

1 1/2 tablespoons whipping
cream

Chive sprouts or pea shoots
for garnish

2 slices toasted country
bread

SERVES 4

With an egg-cutting device, gently clip the top of the egg shells. Pour the eggs into a bowl. Trim the shells with scissors if needed. Rinse the shells under cold water and set aside on egg holders.

In a small sauce pot, heat the butter and gently cook the shallots without browning. Add the eggs and cook over medium heat, whisking the entire time. Add the salt and pepper. Do not let the eggs brown or get fluffy. When the eggs start to pull together, add the sliced truffles and whipping cream.

Remove the eggs from the heat and gently spoon the truffled egg mix into the shells. Garnish with truffles and sprouts or pea shoots.

Serve with toasted country bread.

You might want to strain the eggs. You'll probably get some shell when making this recipe. Also make sure you have some small spoons available to get down into the shell.

MICHELLE'S HOE CAKES

DRY INGREDIENTS

1 cup white cornmeal

1 cup all-purpose flour

3 teaspoons baking powder

2 teaspoons salt

4 cranks fresh-ground
   white pepper

WET INGREDIENTS

3 eggs

1 cup buttermilk

1/3 cup crème fraiche

1 cup cooked corn kernels

1/3 cup finely chopped
   shallots

4 tablespoons unsalted
   butter, melted

1 tablespoon butter, divided

4 ounces breakfast sausage,
   formed into 2 round patties

2 large eggs

1/2 teaspoon salt

2 cranks fresh-ground
   white pepper

1/4 bunch chives

SERVES 2

Sift together the dry ingredients. In a second bowl, mix the wet ingredients.

Make a well in the dry ingredients and pour the wet ingredients into the well. Mix lightly to incorporate all ingredients.

In a small Teflon pan, heat 1/2 tablespoon butter. Spoon in 2 tablespoons hoe-cake mix and cook over medium heat. As it cooks, it will pull together. Flip like a small pancake and brown the other side. Repeat for the other hoe cakes. (This batter will make approximately 20 silver dollar-size hoe cakes.) Keep warm in the oven at 300 degrees.

In another pan, sear the sausage patties for 2 minutes on each side. Remove the patties and fry the two eggs, sunny side up to your liking. Sprinkle with 1/4 teaspoon salt and 1 crank of pepper for each egg.

Place a hoe cake in the center of each plate. Place one sausage on top of each hoe cake. Place one egg on top of the sausage. Finish with chives.

Vegetables

COLLARD GREENS BRAISED IN PALMETTO AMBER BEER

1 pound smoke-house
   bacon, diced small

3 cups finely diced
   Vidalia onions

1/2 cup finely chopped garlic

5 pounds chopped collard
   greens, washed and ribs
   removed

1 gallon chicken stock

3 bottles Palmetto Amber
   beer (or your own favorite)

1 pound ham hock

1/2 cup red wine vinegar

1 tablespoon Old Bay
   seasoning

2 teaspoons celery seeds

4 teaspoons granulated sugar

2 teaspoons salt

6 to 8 cranks fresh-ground
   white pepper

SERVES 6-8

Render the bacon in a heavy-bottomed stockpot until semi-crisp. Add onions and garlic and cook until soft. Add the collard greens and cook for 2 minutes.

Add the chicken stock, beer and remaining ingredients except the salt and pepper. Cook mixture over medium heat for 2 hours or until the greens are soft and pliable.

Serve in a large casserole dish or in small individual dishes as shown in the photo. Add salt and pepper to taste.

I enjoy the natural hearty flavor of the greens. True Southerners drizzle vinegar on top just before serving. In the restaurant, we use leftover reduction sauce from the Kobe Beef Cheek recipe (see page 144) instead of vinegar.

BAKED ANSON MILLS STONE-GROUND GRITS WITH SUN-DRIED TOMATOES & FRESH GOAT CHEESE

2 1/4 cups chicken stock

2 1/2 tablespoons unsalted butter

1/2 cup stone-ground grits

1 to 2 cups heavy cream, divided

1 tablespoon salt

4 cranks fresh-cracked white pepper

2 teaspoons chopped garlic

1 teaspoon fresh thyme

1/2 cup diced sun-dried tomatoes

3/4 cup goat cheese

Chives, chopped (for garnish)

SERVES 2–4

Preheat oven to 350 degrees.

Bring the chicken stock and butter to a boil in a thick-bottomed saucepan. Stir in the grits and return to a boil. Reduce the heat, allowing the grits to cook for 15 minutes at a low boil, until the grits are thick and have absorbed most of the chicken stock. Stir occasionally to keep the grits from sticking.

Add 1/2 cup of the heavy cream to the pot and reduce the heat, allowing the grits to cook slowly for another 10 minutes. As the liquid is absorbed, add more cream. Add salt and pepper. After cooking at least an hour, the grits should be thick and full bodied.

Fold in the garlic, thyme and tomatoes. Crumble the goat cheese on top.

Bake in oven for 6 to 8 minutes. Garnish with chives. Serve very hot!

TIP: Some goat cheeses can be salty. Try them first to adapt the amount of salt to add to this recipe.

You can make this recipe in advance. Pop it in the oven for a few extra minutes to heat it before serving.

ROASTED CORN WITH SMOKED BACON
& CARAMELIZED VIDALIA ONIONS

2 cups roasted corn
(from 12 ears of corn)
removed from cob and
separated (see right)

5 medium Vidalia onions for
1/2 cup caramelized onions

1/4 cup apple-smoked bacon,
diced medium

1/2 teaspoon salt

4 cranks fresh-ground
white pepper

1 tablespoon butter

1/2 bunch chives for garnish

SERVES 4

Grill ears of corn in their husks on your outdoor grill until charred. Remove from heat and cool. Remove the husks and cut corn away from cob, separating them into individual kernels.

Thinly slice the onions. Heat a skillet and brown the onions over medium heat. Lower the heat and simmer until completely cooked and excess liquid is evaporated, approximately 20 to 30 minutes. Salt and pepper to taste.

In an iron skillet, cook the bacon over moderate heat until well browned. Remove excess fat. Toss in the corn and lightly brown for 1 minute. Add the caramelized onions, salt, pepper and butter.

Garnish with finely chopped chives.

Canned corn doesn't work for this recipe, as the kernels fall through the grill slats.

This side dish goes with just about any meat or bird dish and is a great addition to any buffet.

FENNEL PARMESAN GRATIN

3 large heads fresh fennel,
    tops cut off and set aside

1/2 cup white wine

2 bay leaves

3 1/2 tablespoons salt,
    divided

1 tablespoon butter
    (for Pyrex dish)

5 cloves garlic, chopped

6 cranks fresh-ground
    white pepper

1 cup fresh heavy cream

1 1/2 cups grated Parmesan
    cheese

SERVES 4-6

Preheat oven to 350 degrees.

Cover the fennel bulbs with water. Add the wine, bay leaves, and 2 tablespoons salt. Simmer about 20 minutes until cooked completely through (test with a knife).

Remove the fennel bulbs and let cool. Slice into 1/4-inch slices and arrange in a buttered Pyrex dish. Sprinkle with garlic and the rest of the salt and pepper. Pour the cream over the top and bake for approximately 20 minutes.

Remove the dish from the oven and add the Parmesan cheese. Return to the oven and continue baking for another 15 to 20 minutes. Garnish with the green tops of the fennel.

To make this dish even better, add fried oysters from page 102 as shown in the photo.

ROASTED GOLDEN BEETS SCENTED WITH
GRAND MARNIER & MICRO CHIVES

16 small young golden beets, with skin

1 cup vegetable oil

2 1/2 cups water

4 tablespoons unsalted butter, divided

1 tablespoon salt

3 cranks fresh-ground white pepper

1/4 cup Grand Marnier

1 1/2 cups freshly squeezed orange juice

40 micro chives

SERVES 4

Preheat oven to 325 degrees.

Rinse the beets under cold running water. In a large bowl, pour oil over the beets and roll them in your hands to completely cover each. Next, transfer them to a roasting pan with the water, and cover with aluminum foil. Bake for 1 1/2 hours until tender. Remove from oven and let cool.

Once cool to the touch, squeeze the beets to remove the skins and discard them. Cut the beets in half and set aside.

In a large sauté pan, heat 2 tablespoons butter over medium heat. Once the butter has melted, add the beets, salt and pepper. Watch the heat, because you want them to start to lightly brown; once they have turned lightly brown, turn them over or give them a light flip in the pan.

Remove the pan from the flame and add the Grand Marnier. Return the pan to the flame (it may light up—that's OK). Next add the orange juice and cook until reduced by half. Reduce the flame to low and gently stir in the remaining butter. Taste to see if salt and pepper are needed. Serve in small side dishes and garnish with the chives.

RUSSET POTATO, SMOKED BACON
& FRESH THYME GRATIN

2 pounds russet potatoes

1 tablespoon melted butter

3 cloves garlic, chopped fine

1/2 cup cooked smoked
bacon, diced and rendered

3 tablespoons fresh thyme
leaves

1 1/2 tablespoons kosher salt

6 cranks fresh-ground
white pepper

Approximately 3 cups milk

1/2 cup heavy cream

3 tablespoons unsalted
butter, chilled and cut into
small pieces

SERVES 6

Preheat oven to 350 degrees.

Thinly slice potatoes on a mandolin or with a sharp knife. Using the melted butter, grease a 9 1/2 x 6-inch pan. Cover the bottom of the pan with the garlic and layer the potatoes, bacon and thyme. Salt and pepper each layer and save some of the thyme and bacon as a garnish for the top.

Pour enough milk into the pan to cover the potatoes. You may not need to use all the milk. Next, pour the heavy cream on top of the potatoes and place small pieces of the chilled butter on top of the cream.

Bake uncovered for 60 to 80 minutes. Cook until the milk and cream have been absorbed and the potatoes are knife tender. Since all ovens are not calibrated the same, you may have to cover this dish with foil once you have reached a beautiful crusty brown topping.

During the cooking process, the milk cooks and spreads the garlic flavor throughout the dish, so you do not need to layer the garlic.

Vegetables

VEGETABLE PEARLS

2 medium green zucchini

2 medium yellow zucchini

2 turnips, peeled

2 rutabagas, peeled

2 carrots, peeled

2 red beets, peeled and
kept away from the other
vegetables

2 tablespoons unsalted butter
(Plugra, if possible), divided

7 3/4 tablespoons kosher salt,
divided

4 to 5 cranks fresh-ground
white pepper

SERVES 4

Rinse all vegetables under cold water and pat dry with a towel. With a very small melon baller, press into the vegetables and turn to make small vegetable pearls. Sometimes you'll need to gently tap on the side of a bowl to remove the small vegetable ball from the melon baller. Once all vegetables have been made into little balls and kept separate, you will need to blanch them.

Heat 3 small pots of water with 2 tablespoons of salt in each. Bring them all to a boil and keep them over a full flame. Cook the yellow and green zucchini together, and turnips and rutabagas together.

Save 1 pot to cook the carrots. When they are done, remove them with a slotted spoon, and then in the same pot cook the red beets, keeping them apart so they don't bleed juice onto the others. Each batch of vegetables should be blanched for only 15 seconds, then dropped into ice water to stop the cooking and retain color. Once cold, remove the vegetables from the ice water.

In a large sauté pan, heat 1 1/2 tablespoons butter and toss in all the vegetable pearls except the red beets. Sprinkle 1 1/2 tablespoons salt and 3 to 4 cranks pepper on the vegetable pearls. Cook over medium heat for 2 minutes.

In a small sauté pan, heat 1/2 tablespoon butter and cook the red beets with 1/2 teaspoon salt and 1 crank pepper. Sprinkle them over the other vegetables and serve.

Okay, it's a little tedious, but a very memorable dish for your dinner party.

SUNCHOKES & HARICOTS VERTS

9 1/2 tablespoons kosher salt, divided

1 pound sunchokes, peeled (also known as Jerusalem artichokes)

1 pound thin haricots verts

1/4 cup vegetable oil (I prefer grapeseed)

2 tablespoons unsalted butter

2 shallots, chopped

8 medium cloves garlic, peeled and finely diced

3 cranks fresh-ground white pepper

3 tablespoons flat-leaf parsley, rinsed under cold water, roughly chopped

SERVES 4

In a large stainless pot, boil 3 cups water with 3 tablespoons salt. Drop the sunchokes in and cook them until knife tender in the center. Remove the sunchokes and chill quickly in ice water. Once chilled, remove and let dry on a towel.

In another large stainless pot, boil 3 quarts water with 5 tablespoons of salt and cook the haricots verts. Keep the flame on high—the goal is to keep the water boiling so the beans cook as quickly as possible. Cook them past al dente (don't want any crunch, but not mushy—just tender). Remove them and chill in a large ice water bath to stop them from cooking more. Once cool, remove the beans and pat dry. Split each one in half by pinching.

Now that the sunchokes are blanched and chilled, cut them into walnut-sized pieces. In a large sauté pan, heat the oil. Once almost smoking, gently add the sunchoke pieces, and let them brown nicely over medium heat for 3 to 5 minutes. Gently turn them as they brown.

Add the butter and reduce heat to medium. Once the butter is melted, add the shallots and garlic and cook almost a minute without browning; just sweat them.

Add all of the haricots verts, and toss them (if you can) in the pan or gently turn them in the pan with tongs. Season with remaining salt and peppermill. Toss in the parsley, cook another 30 seconds and serve hot!

This is a great side dish for meats, game, wild turkey, or whatever else your husband may have shot.

GRILLED OKRA WITH MAÎTRE D' BUTTER

1 cup unsalted butter,
  room temperature

1 small shallot, chopped fine

2 teaspoons finely chopped
  garlic

3 heaping teaspoons chervil,
  leaves picked

5 heaping teaspoons parsley,
  leaves picked only

2 teaspoons cognac

4 teaspoons white wine
  (Chardonnay or
  Sauvignon Blanc)

1 1/2 teaspoons salt

1 1/2 teaspoons fresh-ground
  white pepper

OKRA

16 pieces baby green okra,
  rinsed under cold water

1/4 cup grapeseed oil or
  vegetable oil (to toss in
  for grilling)

1 tablespoon salt

3 cranks fresh-ground
  white pepper

SERVES 2

This is an easy southern side dish and okra isn't slimy!

To make the Maitre d' Butter, mix all ingredients together in your mixer. If you make this the day before, wrap well before placing in your refrigerator so the garlic odor doesn't spread.

Toss all the baby okra into a large bowl with the oil. Add salt and pepper.

Preheat your outdoor grill and place the okra on the grill with a pair of tongs. Turn the okra as grill marks appear. They should be fully cooked in 3 to 4 minutes.

Place the cooked okra on a serving dish and spoon 2 tablespoons of Maître d' Butter over and around them.

BABY TURNIPS BRAISED IN PORT

4 tablespoons unsalted
  butter, divided

20 baby turnips, peeled and
  cut in half

1 1/2 tablespoons salt

3 cranks fresh-ground
  white pepper

2 shallots, chopped fine

1 bottle port (red, not so
  expensive)

SERVES 4

Place 2 tablespoons butter in a large sauté pan over medium heat. Once melted, add the turnip halves, salt and pepper.

Stir and toss gently to lightly brown. Drop the temperature if needed so the butter doesn't burn. Add shallots and cook for 2 to 3 minutes, then deglaze the pan by adding the bottle of port.

Slowly simmer the port and turnips until the turnips are cooked knife tender. Spoon out the turnips and reduce the port down to 1/2 cup of liquid.

Whisk in the remaining butter. Toss the turnips back in with the port. Re-season with salt and pepper, if necessary.

I love the sweetness with the bite of the turnip. It's great with venison.

CHANTERELLES, SNOW PEAS & PISTACHIOS

20 medium-sized
chanterelle mushrooms

20 snow peas, strings
removed

3 tablespoons whole
unsalted butter, divided

2 shallots, chopped fine

1/2 cup roasted pistachios

1 tablespoon fresh thyme
leaves

1 1/2 tablespoons salt

3 cranks fresh-ground
white pepper

SERVES 4

Cut off the bottoms of the mushrooms and scrape the stems. Rinse only if extremely dirty and dry on a towel. Cut the mushrooms in half lengthwise.

To remove the strings from the snow peas, pull the stems from one end to the other. Blanch the peas in boiling, salted water (2 tablespoons per quart of water) for approximately 30 seconds, then chill in ice water. Once chilled, drain and set aside.

In a large sauté pan, heat 2 tablespoons butter over medium-high heat. Toss in the chanterelles and cook for 1 minute, shaking gently or turning them as they sear lightly.

Add the shallots and cook another 30 seconds. Do not let the shallots brown (reduce the temperature if needed).

Toss in the blanched snow peas, pistachios, thyme, salt and pepper. Finish with the last tablespoon of butter to coat all the vegetables. Serve hot. Taste before serving and re-season if necessary.

One of my favorite things in the world of food is fresh mushrooms when they are at their best . . . it doesn't get any better.

SALADS

SOFT-SHELL CRAB SALAD

CRAB SALAD

2 tablespoons vegetable oil

2 live soft-shell crabs, gills and tail removed

1/2 teaspoon salt

2 cranks fresh-ground white pepper

2 tablespoons all-purpose flour

1 tablespoon butter

3 ounces mixed baby green salads (for the best flavor, get these at the farmers market)

SAUCE

1 shallot, chopped

1/2 cup dry Chardonnay

1/2 cup heavy whipping cream

15 green peppercorns

2 teaspoons salt

3 cranks fresh-ground white pepper

1 tablespoon Dijon mustard

1 tablespoon chopped fresh rosemary

6 white asparagus, blanched

1 tablespoon red ribbon sorrel for garnish

SERVES 2

Preheat oven to 350 degrees.

To make the crab salad, in a medium-sized skillet, heat the vegetable oil over medium-high heat.

Toss the crabs with the salt and pepper and then in flour. Transfer the crabs from one hand to the other to remove excess flour.

Once the oil is hot, place the crabs (back side down) into the pan and reduce to medium heat. Add the butter and cook over medium heat for 1 1/2 minutes, then turn the crabs over and cook the other sides for another minute.

TIP: Sometimes the crabs will blow up like little crab balloons. Prick them with a sharp paring knife to release the air and save your nice shirt from a major splattering if they were to pop.

When the crabs are cooked, remove them from the pan and place in the oven to keep warm.

Add the shallot and wine to the pan you used to cook the crab. Reduce by half. Add the cream and green peppercorns, reducing to almost sauce consistency. Add the salt and pepper. Then stir in the mustard, rosemary and asparagus.

Place the baby greens on a plate. Remove the asparagus from the sauce and lay 3 asparagus spears across each salad. Remove the sautéed crab from the oven and place over the salad. Drizzle 2 tablespoons of sauce over the crab salads. Garnish with red ribbon sorrel and enjoy.

If you haven't had the opportunity to try soft-shell crabs, you have missed out on some Southern love.

WINE PAIRING

Domaine des Berthiers Pouilly Fumé 2003

CHILLED SOUTHERN SMOKED CHICKEN, ENDIVE & CAROLINA SHRIMP SALAD IN A YOGURT & VIRGIN WALNUT OIL SAUCE

SALAD

2 to 3 pounds smoked (cooked) chicken (ask your butcher or supermarket to order this)

2 tablespoons salt

6 cranks fresh-ground white pepper

16 medium-sized fresh shrimp, peeled and deveined

3 tablespoons olive oil, divided

6 heads Belgian endive (keep 1 head of whole leaves for decorating)

24 pieces walnut halves

1 bunch fresh chives, diced fine

SAUCE

1 cup plain yogurt, unsweetened

1/2 lemon, juiced

1 teaspoon salt

3 cranks fresh-ground white pepper

1/4 cup walnut oil (buy the best, French if possible)

SERVES 4

Remove and discard the skin from the chicken. Pull the meat from the bones and remove all cartilage and small tendons. Cut the chicken into long strips and refrigerate to keep chilled.

Salt and pepper the shrimp on both sides. Heat 1 1/2 tablespoons olive oil in a large skillet and sauté 8 of the shrimp over high heat, stirring often, to a light brown for 2 to 3 minutes. Repeat for remaining 8 shrimp. Separating the shrimp into two cooking stages ensures a sear on all sides without crowding the pan.

Cook the shrimp to medium-rare (that's when they are most tender and flavorful). Remove the cooked shrimp from the pan and chill in the refrigerator for 10 minutes.

Cut 1/4 inch off the bottom of each endive. Set aside 1 whole endive head. Slice the remaining endive heads in half lengthwise and cut each half into long strips.

In a bowl, mix together the julienne strips of chicken, endive, walnuts and the shrimp.

To make the yogurt sauce, place the yogurt in a small bowl and whisk in the lemon juice. Add salt and pepper and slowly whisk in the walnut oil, drop by drop.

Mix the yogurt sauce with the chicken mixture; this salad does have more sauce than most salads.

Arrange 3 whole endive leaves on the platter and place the chicken salad mix on top.

Sprinkle with the chopped chives and serve.

A refreshing change from your aunt's chicken salad, and this recipe almost sounds healthy!

WINE PAIRING

Gramona Gessami, Penedès 2003

CAMEMBERT, MARINATED GRAPES, ROASTED PECANS & YOUNG ARUGULA IN A SHERRY VINEGAR & VIRGIN PECAN OIL DRESSING

1 1/2 teaspoons salt

3 cranks fresh-ground
white pepper

2 tablespoons sherry vinegar

6 tablespoons virgin
pecan oil

20 red seedless grapes,
cut in half or 1 pint of champagne grapes

6 ounces fresh young arugula

1 medium-sized French
Camembert cheese, cut
into 1-inch pieces
(Camembert is found at
your high-end supermarket;
keep the Camembert at
room
temperature for better
flavor in this salad.)

1/2 cup roasted pecans

Edible orchid leaves
and sprouts

SERVES 2

In a large bowl, add salt and pepper to the sherry vinegar until the salt is dissolved. Add the pecan oil and then toss in the grape halves to marinate for 5 minutes.

Arrange the arugula on two plates.

Add the Camembert pieces to the vinaigrette.

Sprinkle the roasted pecans over the arugula and spoon the Camembert pieces and grape halves over the salad. Lightly spoon some of the vinaigrette over each salad and garnish with edible orchid leaves and sprouts.

WINE PAIRING

Chateau Ste. Michelle & Dr. Loosen Eroica, Columbia Valley 2004

CHARLESTON GRILL'S CHILLED ROAST DUCK BREAST SALAD WITH PENCIL ASPARAGUS & POACHED BUTTON MUSHROOMS OVER YOUNG SPINACH & DUCK CRACKLINGS

DUCK BREAST SALAD

1 large Long Island duck breast

3 teaspoons salt

5 cranks fresh-ground white pepper

5 tablespoons vegetable oil, divided

16 small fresh button mushrooms

1 shallot, chopped fine

2 cloves garlic, chopped fine

1/4 cup dry white wine (Sauvignon Blanc or Chardonnay)

1 tablespoon lemon juice

12 green pencil size asparagus

6 ounces fresh baby spinach leaves

1 tablespoon finely chopped fresh thyme leaves

VINAIGRETTE

2 tablespoons fresh-squeezed lemon juice

1 1/2 teaspoons salt

3 cranks fresh-ground white pepper

4 tablespoons white truffle oil (Italian or French)

Any edible flower for garnish

SERVES 2

Remove the skin from the duck breast. Cut the skin into julienne strips and set aside. Salt and pepper each side of the duck breast, using 1/2 teaspoon salt and 1 crank of pepper for each side.

Heat a small pan with 1 tablespoon of the vegetable oil. Add the duck breast and sear over medium-high heat for 1 1/2 minutes on each side. Discard the oil. Remove the duck breast from the pan and refrigerate the breast for 20 minutes.

In the same pan, add remaining oil and cook the duck skin slices over a low heat for approximately 20 to 30 minutes until brown and crunchy. Remove the skin from the pan and dry on a paper towel. Discard the oil or save to sear items in other recipes.

In a large sauté pan, heat 2 tablespoons oil over medium-high heat. Add the button mushrooms, tossing them lightly to let them lightly brown, approximately 2 minutes.

Add the shallot, garlic, 2 teaspoons salt and 3 cranks of pepper. Reduce the heat to low. Cook for another minute without browning the shallots. Add the wine and lemon juice to the pan.

Remove from the heat and set aside to marinate for 15 minutes in the refrigerator. Remove the chilled duck breast from the refrigerator and slice as thin as you can, widthwise. Chill.

Blanch the asparagus in boiling, salted water until knife tender. Then chill quickly in ice water, drain and set aside.

To prepare the vinaigrette, add the lemon juice, salt and pepper to a small bowl. Stir to dissolve the salt. Add the truffle oil.

Remove the mushrooms from the marinade and discard the marinade.

In a large bowl, mix together the spinach, asparagus, marinated mushrooms, duck skins, fresh thyme, and the thinly sliced duck breast. Add the vinaigrette and toss gently so all of the items will be seasoned. Place small

mounds of the mixed salad in the center of each plate and rearrange the duck, asparagus, and cracklins over the top for presentation.

Arrange some edible flowers on top of the salad and serve as soon as possible.

I enjoy duck breast tender at medium-rare even in this chilled salad. If you're a little squeamish about medium-rare duck, cook the breast 3 minutes each side over medium heat.

TIP: Always squeeze the lemons at the last second to keep the fresh lemon flavor. Go easy on the truffle oil, as it's best when you only taste a hint of it.

WINE PAIRING

Schramsberg Blanc de Noirs, California 2003

BABY LOLA ROSA LEAVES WITH CLEMSON BLUE CHEESE, MARINATED SHIITAKES & ROASTED HAZELNUTS IN A SWEET PORT & FRESH ROSEMARY SAUCE

SALAD

5 shiitake mushrooms

6 tablespoons olive oil, divided

1 tablespoon balsamic vinegar

25 hazelnuts, toasted

12 to 15 Baby Lola Rosa leaves

1 to 2 ounces crumbled Clemson blue cheese or Danish blue cheese

6 sunflower sprouts

Chopped rosemary for garnish

SWEET PORT AND FRESH ROSEMARY SAUCE

2 tablespoons grapeseed oil

4 shallots, chopped

4 cups inexpensive port

1/4 cup grapeseed oil

1 1/2 teaspoons salt

3 cranks fresh-ground white pepper

1/4 teaspoon chopped fresh rosemary

SERVES 4

Preheat oven to 325 degrees.

Quarter the shiitake mushrooms and sauté them in 3 tablespoons olive oil over medium-high heat. Immerse the sautéed mushrooms into the balsamic vinegar and the remaining olive oil. Chill overnight.

Bake the hazelnuts for 5 to 7 minutes. Do not let them brown or they will become bitter.

To make the sauce, heat 2 tablespoons grapeseed oil in a medium-sized saucepan and lightly brown the shallots. Add the port and reduce over medium heat to 1/2 cup. While hot, place the port shallot reduction in a blender, not a food processor, and purée. Slowly pour in the 1/4 cup grapeseed oil to emulsify. Add salt and pepper. Add fresh rosemary. Place in the refrigerator until cold.

Place Lola Rosa leaves in the center of the plates. Top with crumbled cheese and hazelnuts still warm from the oven. Place shiitakes on top with the sunflower sprouts and garnish with rosemary around plate rims.

Spoon the port sauce over the top and across all the salad.

TIP: Grapeseed oil is the only oil I use on this recipe because it will not congeal when refrigerated and has no flavor, so it showcases the port.

WINE PAIRING

Selbach Riesling Fish Label, Mosel 2005

WILD TURKEY BREAST SALAD

2 teaspoons salt

11 cranks fresh-ground white pepper

1/2 cup flour

4 large slices wild turkey breast

1/2 cup grapeseed oil

1 cup olive oil

15 pear tomatoes, red and yellow, split in half

2 shallots, chopped

2 cloves garlic, chopped

2 tablespoons capers

2 lemons, juiced

2 tablespoons tarragon leaves

4 portions mixed greens salad

SERVES 4

Preheat oven to 375 degrees.

Using 1/4 teaspoon of salt and 1 crank of pepper for each side, season and then flour the turkey slices. In a large sauté pan, heat the grapeseed oil and lightly brown each side of the turkey breasts, then bake for 3 minutes.

In another sauté pan, heat 1/4 cup olive oil and add the tomatoes, then the shallots, garlic and capers. Cook for 30 seconds, add the lemon juice and 3 cranks of pepper, and the remaining olive oil and the chopped tarragon. Arrange the salad on a plate, place the breast over the greens and pour the vinaigrette over the top.

I made this recipe on my TV show for Lucas Black in exchange for turkey calling lessons. Now he's got a recipe and I sound like a turkey!

WINE PAIRING

Rockhouse Viognier Hadley's Field, North Carolina 2005

SAUTÉED SNOOK SALAD, ELF MUSHROOMS IN A SHERRY VINEGAR & VIRGIN HAZELNUT VINAIGRETTE

2 tablespoons grapeseed oil

1 1/2 tablespoons salt, divided

4 cranks fresh-ground white pepper, divided

8 ounces fresh snook, cut into 2 equal portions

1 tablespoon unsalted butter

6 ounces fresh elf mushrooms, sliced in 1/4-inch slices

2 tablespoons caramelized red pearl onions

1 large shallot, chopped fine

4 ounces frisée salad, cut, washed and dried

10 pea shoots

VINAIGRETTE

3 tablespoons 20-year-old sherry vinegar

1/2 teaspoon salt

4 cranks pepper

4 tablespoons virgin hazelnut oil

2 tablespoons roasted hazelnuts

SERVES 2

Preheat oven to 400 degrees.

Heat the grapeseed oil in a 10-inch sauté pan over medium heat. Sprinkle 1/2 teaspoon salt and 1 crank of pepper to season each side of the snook fillets. Sear the fillets 1 1/2 minutes on each side. Remove from the pan and place in a pie tin.

Remove the excess oil from the pan and return the pan to the heat. Add the butter. Once it is melted, add the mushrooms, pearl onions, 1 tablespoon salt, and 3 cranks of the peppermill. Cook for 20 seconds. Add the chopped shallot and lower the heat, cooking 10 more seconds. Remove the mushroom shallot mix and place it in the same pie tin as the snook fillets.

Without returning the pan to the heat, add the sherry vinegar, 1/2 teaspoon salt and 4 cranks pepper to the hot pan. Do not breathe in the vinegar. Add the hazelnut oil and nuts to finish the vinaigrette.

Place the pie tin with the snook and mushrooms in the oven for 2 minutes.

Arrange the frisée and pea shoots across the center of the plate. Lay the hot fish and mushrooms across the salad and spoon the warm vinaigrette with hazelnuts across the fish.

You can't buy this fish. You'll have to catch it yourself on a fishing trip to Florida. Believe me, you won't be disappointed. It will absolutely not work with any other fish.

WINE PAIRING

Adelsheim Pinot Gris, Oregon 2005

FRIED LOWCOUNTRY OYSTER & WHITE ASPARAGUS SALAD IN A CHARDONNAY, ANCHOVY & ROASTED WALNUT CREAM

SAUCE

3/4 cup Chardonnay wine

2 shallots, chopped fine

5 tablespoons crème fraiche or whipping cream

14 whole walnuts, roasted lightly for 5 minutes at 275 degrees

8 anchovy fillets, drained and chopped

3 cranks fresh-cracked white pepper

Chive sprigs or red ribbon sorrel for garnish

SALAD

4 ounces young frisée salad, cleaned

4 ounces young arugula, cleaned

2 ounces shaved Parmesan cheese

16 baby white asparagus blanched in boiling salted water, then chilled in ice water

OYSTER BATTER

2 quarts frying oil

1 cup flour

1/2 tablespoon Old Bay seasoning

1 teaspoon salt

4 cranks fresh-cracked white pepper

10 oysters, shucked (save the liquid inside the shells)

SERVES 2

To prepare the sauce, heat the white wine and shallots in a small saucepan and reduce over a medium flame to 1/4 cup liquid. Add the crème fraiche and reduce to a sauce consistency. Add the walnuts, anchovies and pepper. The anchovies may provide enough salt for the sauce.

Arrange the lettuces mixed together on the plate. Sprinkle the shaved Parmesan and lay the asparagus across the leaves.

To prepare the oysters, heat the frying oil to 375 degrees in a deep pot.

Mix the flour, Old Bay seasoning, salt and pepper. Keeping as much juice on the oysters as possible to hold the flour, gently toss the oysters with the Old Bay flour mix. Gently drop the oysters in the hot fat with a skimmer and fry for approximately 10 to 20 seconds. Place the oysters on the salad and spoon some sauce over the top. Serve quickly. Garnish with chive sprigs or red ribbon sorrel.

WINE PAIRING

Havens Albariño, Carneros 2002

GRILLED ASPARAGUS, SMOKED SALMON & GRAPEFRUIT SALAD IN A CITRUS PINK PEPPERCORN VINAIGRETTE

12 pencil asparagus, blanched (keep the rubber bands on the bunch of asparagus and cut 2 inches off the bottom before blanching)

1 tablespoon vegetable oil

4 1/2 tablespoons salt

4 cranks fresh-ground white pepper

2 limes, juiced

1 teaspoon pink peppercorns

6 tablespoons virgin olive oil

1 shallot, chopped

1 tablespoon chopped fresh chives

4 slices high-quality smoked salmon

2 large ripe grapefruits, peeled and segments removed

6 baby cuc-a-melons

SERVES 2

Heat your grill.

To blanch the asparagus, boil 1 gallon of water in a stainless steel pot with 3 1/2 tablespoons of salt. This should almost taste like seawater. Bring to a boil over high heat, uncovered. Drop asparagus into boiling water. The water should not stop boiling. Boil approximately 15 seconds, depending on the thickness of the asparagus.

NOTE: It's better to use a large pot with lots of water than a small pot with little water so that the asparagus will retain color and flavor.

Lightly toss the blanched asparagus in the vegetable oil and add the 1/2 tablespoon salt and 2 cranks of white pepper. Grill the asparagus for 1 to 2 minutes on each side and then chill.

For the vinaigrette, in a small bowl add 1/2 tablespoon salt and 3 cranks of pepper to the lime juice. Stir until the salt is dissolved. Add the pink peppercorns, olive oil, shallot and chives.

In the center of each of two plates, layer folds of smoked salmon, asparagus, grapefruit segments and baby cuc-a-melons. Drizzle some vinaigrette over the salad. Serve very cold.

When buying smoked salmon, you get what you pay for. Cheap salmon means cheap flavor.

WINE PAIRING

Château La Louvière, Pessac-Léognan 2002

WARM SALMON SALAD WITH GOAT CHEESE IN A TOMATO & FRESH CILANTRO BUTTER

TOMATO AND FRESH CILANTRO BUTTER

2 1/2 cups white wine

2 shallots, chopped fine

1/4 pound butter, cut into cubes

1 1/2 teaspoons salt

3 cranks fresh-ground white pepper

2 tablespoons fresh cilantro leaves, chopped rough

1 1/2 tablespoons coriander seeds

WARM SALMON SALAD

24 ounces fresh salmon, skin and bones removed

1 tablespoon salt

4 cranks pepper

2 tablespoons olive oil

20 cherry tomatoes, cut in half

1/2 pound mixed greens

8 ounces fresh goat cheese, crumbled

To prepare the butter, heat the white wine and shallots in a medium-sized saucepan and reduce to about 1/4 cup liquid. Over a low flame, whisk in the cold butter, little by little to emulsify. Season with salt and pepper to taste and keep warm. If the sauce boils or gets too cold, it will separate and you'll need to start over. Just before serving, add the chopped cilantro and coriander seeds.

Cut the salmon into bite-sized pieces and season with 1 tablespoon salt and 4 cranks pepper. Heat the olive oil in a Teflon pan over a medium-high heat. Add the salmon pieces and sear for 20 seconds on each side. Remove the salmon pieces and set aside.

Add the tomatoes to the Teflon pan and let cook for 30 seconds.

Lay the salad greens flat on the plates and crumble the goat cheese over the salads. Place the salmon and tomatoes evenly across the greens.

Spoon the sauce over the salad (approximately 2 1/2 tablespoons each). Serve quickly. This is one of my favorite warm salads.

WINE PAIRING

Krug Brut Grande Cuvée Champagne

STUFFED PARMA PROSCIUTTO IN A
SHERRY VINEGAR & PECAN OIL VINAIGRETTE

VINAIGRETTE

2/3 cup sherry vinegar

1 teaspoon salt

3 cranks pepper

4 ounces virgin pecan oil (French oils are the best!)

SALAD

4 thin slices prosciutto de parma ham (country ham won't work)

20 roasted pecans baked at 275 degrees for 5 minutes

4 tablespoons goat cheese

20 to 24 sunflower sprouts or frisée salad

Fresh chive sprouts

SERVES 2

To prepare the vinaigrette, in a small saucepan over low heat, reduce the sherry vinegar to 2 tablespoons and add 1 teaspoon salt and 3 cranks pepper. Remove from heat and chill. Add the virgin pecan oil once chilled.

Using a ring mold (or PVC pipe cut 3 inches in diameter, 2 inches high), drape the center of two slices of prosciutto down into the ring mold with the ends halfway over the sides. In the center, place half of the pecans, all the crumbled goat cheese and several sunflower sprouts.

Use 1 tablespoon of vinaigrette to drizzle over the goat cheese and pecans inside the prosciutto ring. Fold prosciutto over on top to form a pouch. Remove the ring mold and arrange the remaining sprouts around the plate in a circle. For two people you will repeat these steps twice.

Finish by sprinkling pecans on the plate and drizzle another tablespoon of dressing around the outside. Top with fresh chive sprouts.

WINE PAIRING

Feudi San Gregorio Falanghina, Campania 2003

ENDIVE & AVOCADO SALAD SCENTED
WITH LIME & PISTACHIO OIL

LIME AND PISTACHIO OIL

3 limes, juiced

1 teaspoon salt

3 cranks fresh-ground
white pepper

3 tablespoons high-quality
olive oil

3 tablespoons pistachio oil
(Mr. Motegoutero oil)

1 teaspoon fresh thyme leaves

MOUSSE

3 ripe avocados

2 shallots, chopped fine

2 small cloves garlic,
chopped fine

2 limes, sliced

1 tablespoon salt

1 crank fresh-ground white
pepper

3 tablespoons pistachios

ENDIVE SALAD

2 heirloom tomatoes, skin
removed and cut into 6
pieces each (burn or blanch
to remove skins)

2 heads Belgium endive

1 bunch chives

4 tablespoons roasted
pistachios for garnish

Sprouts for garnish

Baguettes for garnish

Edible flowers for garnish

SERVES 4

Do not make the sauce in advance; squeezing the limes at the last minute keeps their fresh flavor. Juice the limes, add salt, and dissolve. Add pepper, olive oil, pistachio oil and thyme.

To prepare the mousse, cut the avocados in half and remove the pits. Scoop out the ripe avocado and place in a bowl. Discard the skin. Lightly mash the ripe avocado with a heavy grade whisk. Add the shallots, garlic, lime juice, 1 tablespoon salt, 1 crank pepper and then the pistachios. Keep slightly chunky and wrap in a plastic pastry bag and chill for 1 hour.

For each plate, squeeze 3 small dollops of avocado mousse across the plate in a line. Set a slice of tomato on each of the dollops of avocado mousse and squeeze a dollop of avocado mousse on top of each tomato.

Gently arrange the endive leaves, sprouts, and baguettes (if desired, garnish with chive tips, edible flowers and pistachios). Spoon some of the vinaigrette over the salad and enjoy.

In the restaurant we use thin slices of French bread (baguettes) sprayed with olive oil and baked at 250 degrees until dry. It's more work, but adds a fun crunch to the dish.

WINE PAIRING

Kozlovic´ Malvazija, Croatia 2004

SAUTÉED CHICKEN LIVERS OVER FRISÉE IN A WARM RED WINE VINEGAR & SMOKED BACON VINAIGRETTE

4 ounces slab bacon, diced

1 tablespoon salt

5 cranks fresh-ground white pepper

8 Bresse chicken livers from France (Blondes are the best but are hard to find; try to find pasture-raised chicken livers)

2 1/2 tablespoons vegetable oil, divided

2 medium shallots, chopped fine

3 tablespoons aged red wine vinegar (French if possible)

2 tablespoons chicken demi-glace (reduced chicken stock)

1 tablespoon fresh thyme leaves

1 bunch thin chives (save the tips for garnish)

3 small heads frisée greens, washed

SERVES 2

In a large sauté pan, heat the bacon over medium heat until crispy, approximately 4 minutes. Remove the bacon and set aside.

Salt and pepper all sides of the chicken livers. Quickly sear the livers in the bacon fat over medium heat for 15 seconds on each side. Once seared to medium-rare or medium, remove the livers from the pan and set aside. Discard the leftover fat in the pan.

In the same pan, add 1/2 tablespoon oil and the shallots and gently cook over a low flame for 1 minute (do not brown the shallots). Cook until translucent, then add the red wine vinegar to the pan, and, over low heat, reduce to 1 1/2 tablespoons liquid. Next add the chicken demi-glace, bring the sauce to a simmer, and turn off the heat. Re-season with pepper (careful not to over-season as the bacon will provide a lot of salt) and fresh thyme.

When you're ready to serve, add the seared livers, bacon and chopped chives to the hot reduction.

Add the remaining vegetable oil to the sauce—this is a broken warm vinaigrette, do not reheat this sauce. You want to keep the livers medium-rare.

Arrange the frisée flat across the plates. Gently place the warm livers over the salads and drizzle the warm vinaigrette over the salads. Garnish with chive tips.

Serve at once with grilled country bread.

TIP: You get what you pay for when buying vinegars. The French are great at making vinegar. Remember: great dishes start with great products.

WINE PAIRING

Sass Pinot Noir, Willamette Valley 2005

VEAL SWEETBREADS, WHITE ASPARAGUS & FRIED BLACK TRUMPETS SALAD IN A CITRUS TRUFFLE VINAIGRETTE

VINAIGRETTE

1 teaspoon salt

3 cranks fresh-ground white pepper

1 large lemon, juiced

4 tablespoons white truffle oil

SALAD

8 ounces fresh veal sweetbreads

3 1/2 teaspoons salt, divided

6 cranks fresh-ground white pepper, divided

1 tablespoon grapeseed or vegetable oil

2 tablespoons unsalted butter, divided

8 fresh black trumpet mushrooms

1/2 cup all-purpose flour

1 whole egg, whipped gently

1/2 cup cornmeal

2 cups vegetable oil for frying

6 white asparagus, blanched and chilled

4 ounces mixed farmers market greens, rinsed

Marigold flowers for garnish

SERVES 2

You'll want to make the vinaigrette while the sweetbreads are searing. The longer the fresh juice sits, the less flavor it will have. To make the vinaigrette, add the salt and pepper to the lemon juice. Stir until the salt is dissolved and then add the truffle oil.

With a sharp paring knife, remove any white membrane that surrounds the sweetbreads. Cut the 4 ounces of sweetbreads per person into 3 or 4 pieces; slicing them 1/4 inch thick helps them to cook faster. Using 2 teaspoons of salt and 4 cranks of pepper, season both sides of the sweetbread slices.

In a medium-sized sauté pan over high heat, add 1 tablespoon oil. Once hot, add 1 tablespoon butter. Before the butter browns, add all the sweetbreads. Place the slices side by side but not touching each other.

Drop the temperature to medium and let them do their thing. Do not shake or shimmy the pan; do not move the sweetbread slices. Let them sear until golden brown. You can peek under them after 1 1/2 minutes to see if they are brown. Once browned, flip the sweetbread slices over and try to get the same color on the other side, usually another 2 minutes. Remove the browned sweetbreads from the pan.

Trim the bottoms of the black trumpets and split in half lengthwise. Rinse in cold water and pat dry on a towel. Dip the trumpets in flour, then egg, then cornmeal.

In a large pot, heat the vegetable oil to 350 degrees. Using long tongs or a small fry basket, gently drop the battered black trumpets into the hot oil and fry for 15 to 20 seconds. This is best done in a larger pot than you would choose. Better that than a hot oil accident.

Remove the trumpets from the hot oil and place on a dry towel.

Add the remaining butter to the sweetbread pan and toss in your blanched white asparagus. Sprinkle 1 1/2 teaspoons of salt and 2 cranks of pepper over the asparagus. Whatever you do, don't forget the asparagus, like I did for the photo!

Your goal is to heat the asparagus and get a light brown sear, so cook for only about 1 1/2 minutes.

Toss the sweetbreads back in with the asparagus to heat them.

Arrange the fresh greens on your nicest plates and wander the asparagus and sweetbreads over the salad. Spoon some vinaigrette over everything. Remember: the lemon juice is under the oil on the bottom of the bowl, so dip down to make sure you get the juice as well as the fragrant truffle oil. Garnish with flowers and fried trumpets.

WINE PAIRING
Parusso Barbera d'Alba "Ornati," Piedmont 2003

BRESAOLA, ARUGULA & CÈPES SALAD

6 ounces Bresaola Swiss dried beef tenderloin

3 medium fresh cèpes, cut in half

2 tablespoons butter

2 shallots, chopped fine

6 tablespoons virgin olive oil, divided

5 tablespoons Bangul's vinegar

2 teaspoons salt

4 cranks fresh-ground white pepper

2 tablespoons fresh thyme

4 ounces baby arugula, rinsed

SERVES 2

Ask your specialty shop to slice the Bresaola as thin as possible. Keep it in an airtight container and chilled.

With a paring knife, scrape the mousse from under the cap of the cèpes and discard. Split the cèpes in half to check for critters (sometimes there are small worms).

In a large sauté pan, heat the butter over medium-high heat and add the cèpes, cut side down, to sear and brown without burning. Once brown, gently turn the mushrooms and drop the heat. Cook for another minute and remove the cèpes.

Add the shallots to the same pan with 1 tablespoon olive oil to cook gently without browning for 1 minute. Add the vinegar and reduce to 2 tablespoons liquid. Add the salt and pepper and the remaining olive oil for your vinaigrette.

Toss the cèpes into the warm vinaigrette and add the fresh thyme.

Arrange the Bresaola and baby arugula on plates. Add the warm mushrooms and drizzle the vinaigrette over each salad.

WINE PAIRING

Louis Jadot Fixin Blanc, Burgundy 2003

Soups

CAROLINA CREEK SHRIMP & LOBSTER BISQUE

1/2 cup vegetable oil

2 onions, peeled and diced

3 leek greens, cleaned and cut into 1/4-inch slices

2 carrots, peeled and cut into 1/4-inch rounds

6 lobster heads

1 tablespoon ginger, peeled and chopped fine

Shells from 10 pounds of shrimp

1/2 cup cognac

5 quarts cream

8 sprigs basil

1/2 cup tomato paste

3 to 4 tablespoons salt

10 cranks fresh-ground white pepper

SERVES 16

Preheat oven to 350 degrees.

In a large roasting pan, heat oil over high heat. Add the onions, leeks and carrots.

Bake the lobster heads at 350 degrees for 5 minutes.

Add the ginger, shrimp shells and baked lobster heads to the roasting pan. Sear another 2 minutes. Remove from heat and add the cognac. Be careful of the flambé effect.

Return the roasting pan to the burner and add the cream, basil and tomato paste and simmer for 30 minutes, crushing the lobster heads with a wooden spoon.

Strain the bisque and season with salt and pepper.

For a bonus, garnish with fresh steamed lobster claws, tail meat or wild American shrimp.

Save this one for your family reunion, as this recipe makes a lot.

WINE PAIRING

Lustau Almacenista Manzanilla Pasada de Sanlúcar (Sherry)

CHARLESTON GRILL'S YELLOW TOMATO GAZPACHO
WITH CAROLINA GOAT CHEESE, CUCUMBERS & CILANTRO

5 large yellow tomatoes, stems removed and quartered (buy the ripest, even over-ripe, heirloom yellow tomatoes you can find)

1 medium onion, chopped

2 shallots, chopped

1 large clove garlic, minced

1 1/2 tablespoons kosher salt

4 or 5 cranks fresh-ground white pepper

1 small seeded yellow bell pepper, chopped

2 tablespoons extra-virgin olive oil

6 tablespoons crumbled fresh goat cheese for garnish

4 tablespoons cucumber, skin on and seeds removed, diced for garnish

8 red pear tomatoes, quartered for garnish

18 cilantro leaves for garnish

SERVES 4

VERY IMPORTANT—the day before serving, mix together all the soup ingredients, except the olive oil, in a large mixing bowl. Mix and purée in a blender in small batches. I find it best to fill the blender halfway with mix and blend until smooth. Drizzle the oil in as you're blending.

Chill the entire mix, as well as your serving bowls, overnight. Before serving, re-season as needed.

Garnish your chilled bowls with the crumbled goat cheese, diced cucumber, pear tomatoes and cilantro.

By the way, lots of people have told me this is not how gazpacho is made. I like to play with my recipes, and since this is my book, this is my recipe.

TIP: You MUST make this soup a day in advance. The raw onion, shallot and garlic are strong flavors and will be harsh the same day, but will mellow and blend into a wonderful soup overnight. If your tomatoes aren't very sweet, add 1 tablespoon of sugar to balance the acidity.

WINE PAIRING

Heidi Schröck Vogelsang, Rust 2005

CHILLED BEET & WATERMELON SOUP

1/2 cup grapeseed oil

1 large onion, peeled and
  sliced

2 pounds peeled beets,
  cut into eighths

1 1/2 tablespoons salt

6 cranks pepper

1 watermelon

1 grapefruit, cut into segments
  and skin removed for garnish

8 mint leaves for garnish

Yellow seedless watermelon
  for garnish (optional)

SERVES 4

In a large, heavy-bottomed pot, heat the oil over medium heat and cook
the onion until translucent (do not brown). Add the beets and sear without
burning, until tender.

Cover the beets and onion with water and cook until well done and
completely tender.

While still hot, pour the beets, water, and onion into a blender and blend
on high speed. Add the salt and pepper and chill in the refrigerator or on ice
until very cold.

Just before serving, juice the watermelon by pressing the skinless watermelon through a fine strainer.

Remove the beet purée from the refrigerator and thin it with the fresh
pressed watermelon juice. Re-season with salt and pepper if necessary.

Garnish this bowl with grapefruit segments, mint and yellow seedless
watermelon.

This is a wonderful chilled soup and although I transformed my
co-author's taste buds, I couldn't give it away at my restaurant in France!

WINE PAIRING

Château Mas Neuf Costières de Nîmes, Southern France 2005

GRILLED CORN SOUP WITH PORK CRACKLINGS, SMOKED BACON & THYME

6 whole yellow ears of corn in the husk

2 tablespoons unsalted butter

1 medium onion, peeled and sliced

2 shallots, peeled and sliced

1 1/2 tablespoons salt

4 cranks fresh-ground white pepper

6 cloves garlic, chopped fine

1 quart chicken stock

2 bay leaves

3 tablespoons fresh thyme leaves, divided

1/2 pint whipping cream

4 tablespoons bacon, cooked dry and crumbled

1 small bag (6 ounces) cracklings

SERVES 4

Heat your outdoor grill and grill the corn in the husk. Cook 3 to 5 minutes, turning as the husk browns. It's okay if it burns. Remove the corn from the grill and let cool. Once the corn is cool, remove the husk by pulling it off. Take a sharp knife and cut the kernels off the cob by holding the corn upright and slicing downward towards the cutting board. Discard the cob and set the kernels aside.

In a large, heavy-bottomed pot (stainless if possible) heat the butter over medium heat and add the sliced onion and shallots. Cook without browning for about 2 minutes. Add salt and pepper and then add the corn kernels and chopped garlic. Cook another 2 minutes. Add the chicken stock, bay leaves and 2 tablespoons thyme leaves. Let simmer 30 minutes. Remove the bay leaves.

While still hot, blend the soup in your blender (not food processor) until very smooth. It helps if you blend only 1/3 of the soup at a time; it takes a little more time but blends better.

Before serving, place the smooth soup in a new pot and bring to a boil. Add the cream and re-season with salt and pepper if necessary. Pour the soup into four hot bowls and garnish with the bacon, remaining thyme and cracklings.

WINE PAIRING

Chalone Chardonnay, Chalone 2003

ROASTED GARLIC SOUP WITH PARMESAN & LEMON THYME

5 ounces garlic cloves
   to roast

1 tablespoon extra-virgin
   olive oil

1 sliced yellow onion
   (sweated in butter)

1 1/2 fresh sprigs thyme

2 tablespoons unsalted butter

3 ounces garlic cloves
   (unroasted)

2 cups blonde chicken stock

1/2 cup heavy cream

Salt and pepper

1 tablespoon grated
   Parmesan cheese, divided

1 lemon wedge

SERVES 4

Preheat the oven to 350 degrees.

Roast garlic in olive oil on a sheet pan for 15 minutes or until light golden brown and soft.

In a medium pan, sweat the onion and thyme in the butter until tender (do not brown). Add the roasted and raw garlic to the onions and cook for another 5 minutes.

Add the chicken stock and let simmer for 30 minutes or until garlic is well done. Add the heavy cream. Pour into a blender and blend until smooth. Add salt and fresh cracked white pepper to taste.

Serve in a warm bowl with 1/4 tablespoon of grated Parmesan cheese in each bowl. Add a wedge of lemon to squeeze into the soup at the last minute.

WINE PAIRING

Whetstone Pinot Noir Hirsch Vineyard, Sonoma Coast 2004

SKILLET-SEARED BUTTON MUSHROOM SOUP
WITH FRESH SUMMER TRUFFLES

1/2 cup butter, divided

2 1/2 pounds button mushrooms, washed and towel dried

6 shallots, peeled and sliced

6 cloves garlic, chopped

1/2 gallon chicken stock, divided

3 stems fresh thyme

1 1/2 tablespoons salt

6 cranks fresh-ground white pepper

6 tablespoons sautéed wild mushrooms

6 teaspoons shaved fresh truffles

SERVES 6

Heat 2 tablespoons butter in a sauté pan until almost brown. Add one-fourth of the button mushrooms and let them brown in the pan without shaking them for 30 seconds. Then shake the pan to toss them around a bit. Remove the mushrooms and set aside. Repeat above steps until all the mushrooms are browned.

In the last pan of mushrooms, add the shallots and garlic and cook for 2 minutes.

De-glaze the pan with 1/2 cup of the chicken stock. Add this juice from the pan and all the mushrooms to a large pot. Cover with the rest of the stock, thyme, salt and pepper. Boil for 15 minutes over a hot flame. Remove the thyme and purée the mixture in a blender until smooth. Add salt and pepper to taste.

Serve very hot over sautéed wild mushrooms and garnish with the shaved truffle.

WINE PAIRING

Jayer-Gilles Cotes de Nuits-Villages 1997

GREEN LENTIL SOUP WITH CRÈME FRAICHE

1 tablespoon vegetable oil

4 ounces sliced bacon, diced
(or 1 ham hock)

1 medium-sized onion,
chopped fine

1 leek, split and washed,
chopped fine

1 medium-sized carrot, peeled
and chopped fine

4 cloves garlic, chopped fine

5 branches fresh thyme
(3 to cook and 2 for gar-
nish)

2 bay leaves

1 pound dry lentils

2 1/2 quarts chicken stock
or water

1 1/2 tablespoons salt

4 cranks fresh-ground
white pepper

1 lemon, juiced

1 tablespoon crème fraiche
or sour cream

SERVES 6

In a large, thick-bottomed pot, heat the vegetable oil and sear the diced bacon until lightly browned. Add the onion, leek and carrot. Cook over medium heat until vegetables are lightly browned.

Add the garlic, thyme, bay leaves and lentils. Cook for another minute, stirring often. Add the water or chicken stock and bring to a boil.

Reduce the heat to low and cook slowly for 1 1/2 hours until completely tender. Remove the thyme and bay leaves and season with salt and pepper.

Purée small amounts at a time in a blender (not a food processor) until smooth. Re-season if necessary. Add the lemon juice just before serving, mixing well.

Serve hot and garnish with the leaves of 2 thyme branches and crème fraiche or sour cream.

This is a great soup for those one or two days of winter in Charleston.

WINE PAIRING

J. Palacious Bierzo Pétalos, Spain 2004

CHILLED CREAM OF CAULIFLOWER SCENTED WITH NUTMEG

1 large head cauliflower, leaves removed and cut into florets

3 tablespoons salt

5 cranks fresh-ground white pepper

2 cups heavy whipping cream, at room temperature

1 tablespoon Dijon mustard

1 nutmeg nut for garnish

1 small purple cauliflower for garnish

SERVES 4

Cover the cauliflower florets with 3 quarts cold water and add 1 1/2 tablespoons salt. Bring the water to a boil and drop to a simmer until the cauliflower is completely cooked through. Drain the cauliflower and, while it is still hot, put in a blender (not a food processor) and blend slowly. Add the salt, pepper and cream in small batches, as it will purée better if you don't fill the blender.

Finish by adding the mustard. Taste and re-season with salt and pepper if necessary.

Chill and taste again, as it will taste different cold. Serve in a super-chilled bowl. Gently grate a small amount of the nutmeg nut on top of each as a garnish and top with a slice of raw or poached purple cauliflower.

Thin or thick, this is a fun soup.

WINE PAIRING

Vilmart Coeur de Cuvee Champagne

CHILLED FENNEL SOUP WITH
WHIPPED DIJON CREAM & DILL

1/2 cup grapeseed oil

1 large onion, sliced

4 bulbs fennel, tops removed
and sliced thin

3 cups Noilly Prat vermouth

1/2 gallon water

1 1/2 tablespoons salt

4 cranks fresh-ground white
pepper

CREAM

1/2 cup whipping cream

1 teaspoon Dijon mustard

1 tablespoon salt

2 cranks fresh-ground white
pepper

1/2 teaspoon dill sprigs

SERVES 4

In a large stainless pot, heat the oil over medium-high heat. Add the onion
and cook 3 minutes to sweat but not brown. Add the fennel slices and cook,
stirring often until limp. Once again, do not brown. Drop the temperature
if needed.

Add the Noilly Prat and bring to a boil. Add the water and simmer for 20
minutes until onion and fennel are completely cooked.

Strain the fennel-onion mix and save the cooking juice. In your kitchen
blender, purée the hot fennel-onion mix and add the cooking liquid to thin
the purée to a soup consistency. Remember: it will thicken as it cools, so save
all the cooking liquid. Add the salt and pepper. Chill in an ice bath.

To make the cream, gently whip the cream to soft peaks. Add the Dijon,
salt and pepper. Spoon some of this into the bottom of the serving bowls and
garnish with the dill sprigs. Pour the chilled fennel soup over the whipped
cream and serve as cold as possible.

If you have any French pastis (aperitif), a drop of this in the soup does
wonders.

WINE PAIRING

Guigal St.-Joseph Blanc St.-Joseph, Veneto 2004

HE-CRAB SOUP

1 cup vegetable oil

8 shallots, sliced

2 branches fresh lemongrass, chopped rough

10 cloves garlic

2 whole leeks, sliced and washed

15 Roma tomatoes, split

15 whole live blue crabs (purge in cold water 1 1/2 hours)

1 bottle Chardonnay wine

1/2 gallon fish fumé (stock)

2 tablespoons tomato paste

3 quarts whipping cream

5 tablespoons salt

8 cranks fresh-ground white pepper

3 to 4 seared pear tomatoes per person for garnish

2 sprigs chervil for garnish

3 to 4 pieces lump crabmeat per person for garnish

A pinch of espolette for garnish (can be found in the gourmet section of finer grocery stores)

SERVES 32

Heat the oil and sear the shallots, lemongrass, garlic and leeks together. Add the tomatoes and sear. Toss in the purged live crabs and cook for 5 minutes, stirring often. Try to crush them up with a wooden spoon while they are cooking.

Deglaze with the wine and fish fumé. Add the tomato paste and simmer for 35 minutes.

Remove the crabs and purée them in the food processor. Yes, puree the shells and all. It's best to use the pulse button on the food processor to chop them up.

Return the purée to the pan and add the cream. Add salt and pepper. Cook another 20 minutes.

Strain the soup and pour into bowls. Serve with sautéed split pear tomatoes, chervil and lump crabmeat pieces sprinkled with espolette.

I was never crazy about making soup out of crab roe (usually frozen). I thought I'd try doing something with the guy crabs. This is the result.

WINE PAIRING

Steele Pinot Blanc, Santa Barbara County 2004

MEAT & GAME

CAROLINA QUAIL WITH COUNTRY-FRIED
FOIE GRAS & SAWMILL GRAVY

QUAIL

1 tablespoon butter

1 tablespoon salt

4 cranks fresh-ground white pepper

2 large Carolina quail, breast and legs removed

GRAVY

1 tablespoon vegetable oil

2 ounces ground breakfast sausage meat, not spicy

1 tablespoon flour

1/2 cup whole milk, at room temperature

1 teaspoon salt

2 cranks fresh-ground white pepper

1 teaspoon fresh thyme leaves

Quail hearts and livers, diced (optional)

FOIE GRAS

1 cup duck fat or vegetable oil for frying the foie gras

2 3-ounce slices raw foie gras (duck liver)

2 teaspoons salt

4 cranks fresh-ground white pepper

3 tablespoons all-purpose flour

1 tablespoon cornstarch

1/4 cup buttermilk

1 ounce micro chives

SERVES 2

Preheat the oven to 400 degrees.

In a medium-sized sauté pan, heat the butter. Sprinkle salt and pepper across the quail breasts and legs. Place the legs and breasts skin side down in the pan and sear over medium heat approximately 2 1/2 minutes to lightly brown the skin. Notice we're not asking you to cook the other side of the quail.

Remove the breasts only and set aside in a pie tin. Leave the legs in the pan and turn them over to cook another 2 1/2 minutes. Remove them and set them with the breasts.

Remove the excess fat from the pan and proceed with the gravy.

For the gravy, heat oil over medium heat and add the ground sausage, cooking 2 to 3 minutes and browning the meat as much as possible. Remove the meat and set aside, leaving the fat in the pan.

Remove the pan from the burner and add the flour. Stir with a wooden spoon. Return to the burner, drop the temperature to low, and cook 1 minute. Add the milk to the flour mixture little by little. Add the salt, pepper and thyme. Return the cooked sausage to the pan. Taste and re-season with salt and pepper if necessary. This will become a thick and pasty gravy sauce. I like it this way for this dish. If you prefer a thinner gravy, add more milk. To make it sexier, dice the quail livers and hearts, sauté them in butter, and add to the gravy just before serving.

To make the foie gras, in a small saucepan, heat the duck fat almost to the smoking point, 375 degrees. Salt each foie gras with 1 teaspoon salt and 2 cranks pepper. Toss the foie gras in the flour and cornstarch, then dip in the buttermilk and then back into the flour and cornstarch.

Gently drop the foie gras into the duck fat, making sure they are some-what submerged. Fry to a light brown, about 1 minute. Gently turn over for about 30 seconds and then remove from the pan.

Pop the quail in the oven for 2 minutes to finish cooking.

Spoon some thick gravy on to each plate. Set the Country-Fried Foie Gras on top of the gravy and place the quail breast on the foie gras. Place the legs to the side. Sprinkle with chives and make an appointment with your heart specialist!

WINE PAIRING
Mongeard-Mugneret Grand Echézeaux Grand Cru 1999

KOBE BEEF CHEEK BRAISED IN PINOT NOIR
WITH BABY CARROTS

12 Kobe beef cheeks, cleaned of silver skin

27 teaspoons salt, divided

54 cranks fresh-ground white pepper, divided

1 1/2 cups oil, divided

2 cups flour

1 pig's foot, split in half, if possible

3 tablespoons butter

3 shallots, chopped fine

1 large leek, chopped fine

1/2 bunch thyme

2 bay leaves

2 carrots, diced

1 orange rind, cut with a knife

8 cloves garlic, chopped fine

2 bottles Pinot Noir

2 pints veal stock demi-glace

1 tablespoon white sugar (if needed)

12 baby carrots, peeled and blanched

SERVES 6

Preheat oven to 350 degrees.

Season each cheek with 1 teaspoon salt and 2 cranks of pepper per side. Heat the largest roasting pot you can find (Le Creuset works best for these braising dishes). Pour in 1 cup oil. As the oil is heating, toss each cheek in the flour and pat off excess flour. Gently place the cheek in the hot oil and brown over medium-high heat on each side. As each cheek browns, remove it from the heat and set aside. Don't heat all the cheeks at the same time. Anything stuck to the bottom of the pot means more flavor for your sauce.

Once all the cheeks have browned, pour the remaining oil into the pot and add the split pig's foot. Brown lightly. Leaving the pig's foot in the pan, discard the excess oil.

Add butter over medium heat and then add the shallots, leek, thyme, bay leaves, carrots, orange rind and garlic. Add 3 tablespoons salt and 6 cranks of pepper and cook gently without burning for 2 minutes over low heat.

De-glaze the pot with the Pinot Noir and bring to a boil. Simmer and reduce by one-third. Add the seared cheeks and veal demi-glace. Place pot in oven and bake for 1 1/2 to 2 hours, uncovered. Stir occasionally so the top layer doesn't burn. It should be slightly simmering in the oven.

Cook gently and slowly until the meat almost falls apart. Gently remove the cheeks from the pot and lay them on a baking sheet. Remove the thyme sprigs, bay leaves, orange rind and pig's foot.

Place the pot on a burner and reduce to a sauce consistency (it should be almost there already). While that's reducing, pick the bones out of the pig's foot to leave only the meat. (Well, it's not really meat, but it's good stuff-just don't tell anyone!) Dice up the good stuff and add it to the sauce in the roasting pan. You now have a magnificent burgundy sauce. At the restaurant, we pour any extra burgundy sauce over collards (see page 65).

Taste the sauce again and if it's a bit tart for your taste, add salt and pepper and 1 tablespoon of white sugar.

Add the meat back to the sauce along with the blanched baby carrots. Gently heat to warm and serve. This dish works well with any braising-style beef cut. The slow cooking time creates tender and flavorful meat. You think it tastes good today, wait to taste the leftovers . . . if there are any!

WINE PAIRING

Penfolds Shiraz Magill Estate, South Australia 2003

SEARED DUCK BREAST IN A SHERRY VINEGAR
LAVENDER HONEY REDUCTION

4 teaspoons salt, divided

4 cranks fresh-ground
white pepper, divided

2 duck breasts, skin removed

3 tablespoons vegetable oil,
divided

20 pearl onions, peeled

1/2 cup sherry vinegar

3 tablespoons lavender honey

1 cup reduced duck stock

1 bay leaf

2 stems fresh thyme

20 seedless grapes, skin
peeled

2 duck livers, chopped into
small pieces (optional)

SERVES 2

Salt and pepper each side of the duck breasts, using 1/2 teaspoon salt and 1 crank of pepper per side.

In a small sauté pan, heat 2 tablespoons oil and sear the duck breasts for 1 1/2 minutes on each side over medium heat. Remove the breasts from the pan and add the pearl onions. Lower the heat and lightly brown the onions, cooking gently for 15 minutes until tender.

Deglaze the pan with the sherry vinegar and reduce by half. Add the honey, duck stock, bay leaf and thyme. Reduce to a sauce consistency and then remove the thyme and bay leaf. Add the breasts back into the sauce along with the peeled grapes. Add salt and pepper to taste.

In a small bowl, mix together remaining oil and the raw chopped duck livers.

When the duck has warmed to a medium-rare, gently stir the duck liver oil mixture into the sauce and simmer for 30 seconds to thicken the sauce and lightly cook the livers. Serve immediately.

To make this dish even more fun, slice the duck skin thin and gently cook it in 2 tablespoons vegetable oil over low heat until brown and crunchy. Sprinkle these cracklins on at the last minute for a little oooh la la!

WINE PAIRING

Saintsbury Pinot Noir Brown Ranch, Carneros 2004

CHARLESTON GRILL POTATO SKINS

SAUSAGE

3 pounds pork shoulder

4 pounds duck breast, skin on

2 pounds unsalted pork fatback

2 cups Grand Marnier

6 tablespoons salt

6 tablespoons pepper

5 tablespoons chopped fresh rosemary

5 tablespoons pink peppercorns

Zest of 5 oranges, diced fine

4 tablespoons fennel seeds, warmed in a pan over medium heat for 1 1/2 minutes

POTATO SKINS

12 slices smoked bacon

1 large Wadmalaw onion, sliced thin

2 cranks fresh-ground white pepper

1 teaspoon salt

6 ounces fresh foie gras, cut into 1/2-ounce pieces

6 small (golf ball-sized) Yukon Gold potatoes

1/2 quart frying oil

1 bunch chives, chopped fine

To prepare the sausage, chop the pork, duck and fatback into 1-inch cubes. Cover with remaining ingredients, wrap, and chill for 3 to 4 hours, or even better, overnight.

Place the grinder attachment and blade in the freezer 1 hour prior to grinding. Grind all of the mix in small batches and transfer to the refrigerator as you grind it to keep the mix as cold as possible.

With your sausage press (I'm sure everyone has one of these), push the mixing through into hog casings. This mix should make about 75 links. If wrapped well, they freeze okay.

Start your grill.

Grill these sausages on your grill for 5 minutes, turning often to gently cook them through. Cut each length into 3 pieces and enjoy them with your Charleston Grill Potato Skins.

Preheat oven to 375 degrees.

To prepare the potato skins, cook the bacon in a heavy-bottomed pan until crispy. Remove the bacon and half of the remaining fat. Add the onion and cook until caramelized.

Season with white pepper only, adding small amounts of water to deglaze if needed.

Add the cooked bacon to the onions and purée in a food processor. Check seasoning.

Salt and pepper the foie gras pieces and sauté them in a small pan, very hot, with no oil added. Cook 5 to 10 seconds on each side. Remove and place on a paper towel.

Cut the potatoes in half and remove the center with a small melon baller.

Heat the frying oil in a pot to 350 degrees and deep fry the potatoes for approximately 3 minutes, until tender.

Spoon some onion-bacon purée into the potato skins. Add 1 piece of foie gras on top. Bake for 3 to 5 minutes.

Remove from oven and sprinkle with chopped chives.

Serve these wonderful little Charleston Grill Potato Skins with your favorite sausages. I enjoy them also with wild boar sausages.

WINE PAIRING
Mas de Fournel Pic Saint Loup, Languedoc 2003

PAN-SEARED VEAL SWEETBREADS IN A MADEIRA
& SUN-DRIED CHERRY REDUCTION

1/4 cup grapeseed oil

7 to 8 shallots, cut in quarters

3/4 cup honey

2 pints blackberries,
  strawberries or raspberries

1 1/4 ounces fresh ginger,
  sliced

1 bottle Madeira

1/4 bottle red wine
  (Pinot Noir)

1/4 cup duck stock, reduced

3 ounces dried cherries,
  covered in boiling hot water
  to plump

SWEETBREADS

1 1/2 tablespoons salt

4 cranks fresh-ground
  white pepper

12 ounces fresh veal
  sweetbreads, cleaned

1 1/2 tablespoons
  unsalted butter

SERVES 2

Preheat oven to 400 degrees.

To make the Madeira reduction, heat the oil and lightly brown the shallots. Add the honey and berries and let cook for a moment. Add the ginger slices.

Deglaze with the Madeira and red wine, reduce to 1 cup liquid and add the duck stock reduction. Purée in a blender. Return this mixture to a small saucepan over low heat. Add the plump cherries and cook 2 minutes to heat the cherries. Set this aside.

Salt and pepper all sides of the sweetbreads. Place the butter in a medium-sized sauté pan and heat over medium-high heat until it's almost brown, then add the sweetbreads. Drop the heat to medium and gently sear the sweetbreads slowly for 3 minutes on each side, browning as much as possible. Remove the sweetbreads from the pan and bake for 5 minutes until very hot.

BONUS: If the sweetbreads pan has not burnt at all, add 1/2 cup of water to the pan after removing the sweetbreads. Cook 2 minutes to reduce and add this juice to your Madeira reduction. Re-season if necessary.

Remove the sweetbreads from the oven and place them in a large, pre-heated serving dish. Spoon the Madeira cherry sauce over each sweetbread, reserving some to pass around to your guests.

This is a great winter dish when good berries are hard to find.

WINE PAIRING

Remoissenet Volnay Santenots 1er Cru 1996

VEAL T-BONE SEARED WITH CÈPES & BABY CARROTS

3 tablespoons grapeseed oil

2 12-ounce veal T-bones

4 teaspoons salt

8 cranks fresh-ground white pepper

2 tablespoons unsalted butter, divided

8 ounces fresh porcini mushrooms, cut in half, soil removed

2 shallots, chopped fine

2 tablespoons cognac

1/2 cup Chardonnay

1/2 cup veal demi-glace

2 tablespoons cream

1 1/2 teaspoons salt

3 cranks fresh-ground white pepper

6 baby carrots, peeled, cut in half and blanched

2 tablespoons fresh chervil leaves

SERVES 2

Preheat oven to 350 degrees.

In a large sauté pan, heat the oil over high heat. Season each side of the T-bones with 1 teaspoon of salt and 2 cranks of pepper. Gently place them in the hot pan and sear them without burning for 1 1/2 minutes each side (remember anything stuck to the pan means flavor for your sauce). Remove the veal from the pan and bake in a cooking pan for 5 minutes (reduce the cooking time for a thinner cut of veal).

Add 1 tablespoon butter to the veal pan. Once melted, toss in the halved mushrooms and cook over medium-high heat, turning them as they brown (approximately 1 minute each side). Once lightly browned, remove the mushrooms and set aside.

Add the shallots and cook gently over low heat for 1 minute and pull the pan off the heat. Add the cognac to deglaze. Wait 10 seconds and then place the pan back over the burner. It may flame a bit, but not as bad as if you'd added the cognac while the pan was still on the burner.

Add the wine and reduce by half. Add the demi-glace and cream along with the salt and pepper. Reduce to a sauce consistency. Add the mushrooms and carrots to the sauce to heat them a bit.

Remove the veal from the oven. If there is any juice in the veal pan, add this to your sauce. Add the chervil.

Place each veal on a plate and spoon the mushrooms and carrots on top. Spoon the sauce over the top and garnish with chervil. If you have any truffles laying around, add them now. Serve hot.

I've always been a meat and wild mushroom guy.

WINE PAIRING

LeRoy Vosne-Romanée Les Genevrières 1er Cru 1990

PAN-SEARED LAMB CHOPS IN A NIÇOISE OLIVE, SHALLOT & THYME VINAIGRETTE

2 teaspoons salt

10 cranks fresh-ground white pepper

4 lamb chops, with most of the fat removed

4 tablespoons virgin olive oil, divided

1 shallot, chopped fine

1 clove garlic, chopped fine

1/2 cup diced tomato, skin and seeds removed

20 niçoise olives, pitted and sliced

1 branch thyme leaves

1 teaspoon capers

1 lemon, juiced

SERVES 2

Preheat oven to 350 degrees.

Salt and pepper all sides of the lamb chops, using 1/4 teaspoon salt and 1 crank of pepper on each side.

In a 10-inch sauté pan, over medium heat, bring 1 tablespoon oil up to almost the smoking point and add the lamb chops. Sear all four chops for 1 minute on each side and then bake in the oven for 3 to 5 minutes.

Add the shallot and garlic to the sauté pan and cook over medium heat for 30 seconds. Add the tomatoes, olives, thyme, capers and 2 cranks of pepper. Cook for 1 minute and remove from the pan into a bowl.

Add the lemon juice and remaining oil to the bowl; re-season if necessary. The olives bring salt to this dish, so taste before adding more salt.

Remove the chops from the oven. Spoon the tomato, olive, caper and thyme vinaigrette over the chops.

We use Colorado lamb at the restaurant; I'd choose that over lamb from France.

WINE PAIRING

Shafer Relentless, Napa Valley 2002

POACHED & SEARED VEAL TONGUE IN A
MUSTARD CORNICHON & FRESH TARRAGON SAUCE

VEAL TONGUE

4 tablespoons unsalted
   butter, divided

1 leek, split, washed and diced

4 shallots, peeled and cut
   in half

6 cloves garlic, cut in half

1 carrot, peeled and diced

3 cups dry white wine

4 stems fresh thyme

1 teaspoon ground white
   peppercorns

1 teaspoon salt

2 bay leaves, fresh if possible

8 cups roasted chicken stock

1 veal tongue

SAUCE

3 shallots, chopped

1 cup Chardonnay

1 tablespoon Dijon grain
   mustard

2 tablespoons chopped
   cornichons

2 tablespoons chopped
   tarragon

2 teaspoons salt

4 cranks fresh-ground
   white pepper

1 tablespoon unsalted butter

SERVES 4

In a medium-sized pot, heat 2 tablespoons butter over medium heat. Add the leek and cook 3 to 4 minutes to lightly brown. Add the shallots and garlic and cook for another 2 minutes. Add the carrot and cook for another 2 minutes, stirring often so it doesn't burn. Add the wine, thyme, ground pepper, salt, bay leaves and chicken stock.

Gently set the tongue in the pot and bring to a simmer over low heat (make sure the tongue is completely submerged during the cooking process; otherwise, it may cook unevenly). Simmer, uncovered, for 3 to 4 hours until completely cooked (a small paring knife inserted into the tongue should offer no resistance).

Remove the tongue from the bouillon and set out at room temperature for 10 minutes to cool.

Once the tongue is cool enough to touch, peel off the outer layer of skin from the tongue (this should pull off very easily). Once peeled, chill the tongue for at least 2 hours. Strain the tongue cooking liquid (bouillon) and set aside.

Slice the chilled veal tongue into 1/4-inch slices. In a large Teflon pan, heat the remaining butter and sear the slices of veal tongue for 1 minute on each side over medium heat. Remove the veal tongue and set aside.

To make the sauce, add shallots to the pan and gently cook without browning. Deglaze the pan with the Chardonnay and reduce to 1/4 cup. Add 2 cups of the tongue bouillon and reduce by at least half. (Save the remaining bouillon . . . it makes a great soup base!)

Whisk in the Dijon grain mustard, cornichons, tarragon, salt and pepper. Whisk in the butter to finish the sauce.

Place the tongue slices across a plate and pour the sauce across the top.

Try this one for your next foodie dinner party; just don't tell them what it is. Let's call it pot roast!

WINE PAIRING

Cakebread Chardonnay, Napa Valley 2004

SAUTEED VENISON TENDERLOIN IN A
PORT & HUCKLEBERRY REDUCTION

8 ounces fresh venison tenderloin, cut into 3 medallions

6 teaspoons salt

12 cranks fresh-ground white pepper

3 tablespoons vegetable oil

4 large fresh figs, sliced in quarter-inch rounds, stems removed

2 tablespoons butter, divided

4 shallots, chopped

3 cups port wine

1/2 cup reduced chicken stock

2 tablespoons honey

1 cup fresh huckleberries (may substitute blueberries or blackberries)

Chive tips for garnish

SERVES 2

Preheat oven to 350 degrees.

Season the tenderloin with 1 teaspoon salt and 2 cranks of pepper on each side of each medallion.

Heat the oil in a medium-sized skillet and sear the tenderloin on all sides until brown, but still rare. Slice the tenderloin in half-inch slices and set a slice of fig in between each slice. Push the slices together to reform the tenderloin and bake for 6 minutes to medium-rare. Remove the tenderloin and set aside.

In the same pan, add 1 tablespoon butter and lightly brown the shallots. Deglaze with the port wine and reduce to one-fourth its volume (sauce consistency).

Add the chicken stock and honey. Salt and pepper to taste. Stir in the remaining butter and add the huckleberries. Cook for another 30 seconds to warm the berries.

Pour over the venison. Serve hot!

Garnish with chive tips and break out the biggest red wine you can find from the cellar of one of your wealthiest friends!

WINE PAIRING

Turley Zinfandel Duarte, Contra Costa County 2004

BAKED COUNTRY CRÉPINETTE OF LOCAL RABBIT LOIN, SEARED FOIE GRAS & VIDALIA ONIONS IN A HOLLYWOOD SAUSAGE SAWMILL GRAVY

1 teaspoon salt

3 cranks fresh-ground white pepper

1 3-ounce slice fresh foie gras lobe

1 3-ounce boneless loin of rabbit

1 12-inch square clean caul fat

2 tablespoons caramelized onions

1 tablespoon chopped chives

1 tablespoon vegetable oil

3 ounces fresh-ground pork sausage

1 teaspoon all-purpose flour

1/4 cup whole milk, at room temperature

10 sprigs chive

Preheat oven to 375 degrees.

Salt and pepper the foie gras on each side, using 1/4 teaspoon of salt and 1 crank of pepper for each side. In a hot sauté pan without oil, sear the foie gras quickly (10 seconds on each side). Set aside.

Butterfly the rabbit loin in half lengthwise and season with 1/4 teaspoon salt and 1 crank of pepper each side.

Lay the caul fat out flat like a piece of paper and lay the rabbit loin in the center.

Layer the foie gras, then caramelized onions, then chopped chives. Gently pull the sides of the caul fat over and around the layered rabbit, cutting if necessary.

In a small Teflon pan, heat the oil and sear the underside of the rabbit crépinette to seal the fat in place. Once sealed, slowly turn the crépinette over to sear the other side (approximately 2 minutes each side). Remove the crépinette while still rare and set aside.

In a small saucepan, heat the pork sausage until lightly browned. Remove the meat and set aside. Add the flour to the pan, stirring with a wooden spoon over low heat, approximately 2 minutes.

While continuously stirring, slowly add the milk and cook for another 3 minutes to thicken. Add the sausage back to the pan gravy.

Heat the crépinette in the oven for 5 minutes. Remove from the oven and slice the crépinette in half widthwise. Place the crépinettes in the centers of two salad plates and spoon some of the sauce over the top. Garnish with chives.

WINE PAIRING
Weinbach Riesling Cuvée Théo, Alsace 2000

PAN-SEARED BEEF TENDERLOIN WITH SMOKED BACON, BUTTON MUSHROOMS & ASPARAGUS

2 teaspoons salt

8 cranks fresh-ground white pepper

12 ounces beef tenderloin, cut into four 3-ounce portions

1 tablespoon vegetable oil

2 tablespoons butter, divided

14 medium-sized button mushrooms, quartered

2 shallots, sliced

6 slices smoked bacon, diced and cooked dry

8 green asparagus, blanched

Thyme for garnish

SERVES 2

Salt and pepper each side of the beef medallions, using 1/4 teaspoon salt and 1 crank of pepper for each side.

In a medium-sized sauté pan, heat the oil. Add 1 tablespoon butter to the pan and when it has melted, sear the beef 1 to 2 minutes on each side. Remove the beef from the pan and add the remaining butter to the pan. Lightly brown the mushrooms for 1 minute. Add the shallots and cook for 30 seconds. Add the cooked bacon and cook another 30 seconds.

Add the blanched asparagus and let everything cook together for another 30 seconds. Spoon the vegetable mixture over each beef medallion and sprinkle with fresh thyme.

For the photo, I added 1/4 cup veal stock reduction with the bacon as a sauce. You don't always need sauce with tender cuts like this.

WINE PAIRING

Beringer Cabernet Sauvignon Private Reserve, Napa Valley 2001

CAROLINA SQUAB, SALSAFY & BABY VEGETABLES IN A ROSEMARY & DICED LIVER JUS

SAUCE

All the squab legs and bones from 2 squabs

1/4 cup vegetable oil

2 shallots, peeled and sliced

1/2 small leek, split, rinsed and sliced

1 small carrot, peeled and cut into 1/4-inch rounds

4 thyme branches

2 bay leaves

4 cloves garlic (whole)

4 tablespoons cognac

1/2 bottle white wine (Chardonnay or Sauvignon Blanc)

SQUAB

2 2 1/2-x-2 1/2 cuts puff pastry

2 squab breasts (removed from whole squab—use the rest of the squab for the sauce)

2 teaspoons salt, divided

5 cranks fresh-ground white pepper, divided

2 tablespoons unsalted butter, divided

4 small salsafy, peeled, split and blanched

8 baby carrots, peeled, split in half and blanched

8 white asparagus, peeled, split in half and blanched

2 livers, saved and diced fine (optional)

1 tablespoon chopped rosemary

To make the sauce, roughly chop the squab carcasses and legs. In a large, heavy-bottomed pot, heat the vegetable oil and squab carcasses and legs over medium heat. Let them sear and brown as much as possible, approximately 5 minutes, stirring often. Add the shallots, leek, carrot, thyme, bay leaves and garlic. Let this cook another 2 to 3 minutes.

Deglaze the pan with the cognac. Add the wine and cover the bones with cold water and bring to a quick boil. Let simmer approximately 2 1/2 hours, pushing the bones down into the stock from time to time.

When the stock has reduced to one-fourth of its original volume, strain it and discard the bones and vegetables. This lovely reduction will be your sauce. Set it aside and begin preparing the squab.

Preheat oven to 375 degrees.

Place the puff pastries on a baking sheet and bake for 10 to 20 minutes until puffed up without over browning. Remove from the oven and set aside.

Sprinkle both sides of the squab breasts with 1/4 teaspoon salt and 1 crank of pepper. In a small sauté pan, heat 1 tablespoon butter. Once melted, add the squab breasts, skin side down, and sear over medium heat for approximately 2 minutes. Flip the breasts over and sear for 30 seconds. Remove the breasts from the pan and deglaze the pan with 1 cup of reduced squab stock. Let this simmer down to a sauce consistency.

In another sauté pan, heat remaining butter over medium heat. Add the salsafy, carrots and asparagus with 1 teaspoon salt and 3 cranks of pepper.

Cut the puff pastries in half. Place the bottom halves on each plate and cover with the buttered vegetables. Place the squab breast into the warm sauce for 30 seconds to heat (medium heat). Remove the breast and place over the vegetables. Next add the chopped livers and rosemary to the sauce. Stir for 20 seconds and spoon over the breast and vegetable. Top with the remaining puff pastries and serve quickly.

WINE PAIRING

Qupé Roussanne Bien Nacido Vineyard, Hillside, Santa Maria Valley 2004

SEARED KURABUTA PORK TENDERLOIN
IN A MUSTARD-CHIVE-DIJON CREAM SAUCE

3 teaspoons salt

12 cranks fresh-ground white pepper

6 2-ounce pork tenderloin medallions

1 tablespoon vegetable oil

2 shallots, chopped fine

1/4 cup Chardonnay wine

1/2 cup heavy cream

1 tablespoon Dijon mustard

1 tablespoon chopped chives

SERVES 2

Preheat oven to 400 degrees.

Salt and pepper the pork on all sides, using 1/4 teaspoon and 1 crank of pepper for each side.

In a medium pan, heat oil over high heat. When the oil is almost smoking, add the pork and sear 1 minute on each side. Do not shake the pan; if it sticks, that's more flavor for the sauce. Remove the pork from the pan and set the heat to low.

Add the shallots and cook for 1 minute. Add the wine and reduce to 1 tablespoon of liquid. Add the cream and reduce by half. Stir in the mustard with a whip and add salt and pepper to taste. Add the chopped chives.

Reheat the pork in the oven for 3 minutes and serve with the mustard sauce over the top.

NOTE: Please don't cook the pork well done. Keep the meat medium-rare and it will be wonderful and tender.

WINE PAIRING

Williams Selyem Zinfandel Bacigalupi, Russian River Valley 2003

ROASTED CHICKEN WITH BACON & CARAMELIZED ONIONS IN A JUS OF SEARED MUSHROOMS

4 ounces slab bacon, sliced fine

2 medium onions, sliced fine

2 tablespoons salt, divided

6 cranks fresh-ground white pepper, divided

1/2 cup water

1 bunch chives, chopped fine on a bias (use half for purée and half for the sauce)

1 large roasting chicken

6 tablespoons vegetable oil, divided

1 medium onion, diced

10 button mushrooms, cleaned and cut into 1/8-inch slices

1 tablespoon unsalted butter

SERVES 4

Preheat oven to 400 degrees.

In a medium-sized sauté pan, heat the bacon over low heat until brown. Add the onions and cook until lightly brown (having them stick to the pan is the goal). Add 1 tablespoon salt and 3 cranks of pepper. Once the onions have browned and are sticking to the pan, add the water and scrape the bottom of the pan.

Cook for another 2 to 3 minutes until the water has evaporated and the onions are completely cooked. Add salt and pepper to taste.

While still hot, purée the onions and bacon in a food processor until smooth. Chill the mixture quickly. Once chilled, add half of the chopped chives to the purée. Set aside.

With a small teaspoon, insert the handle of the spoon between the skin and the breast meat of the chicken, gently pushing back and forth to form a small cavity. Do the same for the thighs, being careful not to damage the skin.

Using the same small teaspoon, separate the skin and spread some of the bacon and onion purée between the breast and skin. Do the same with the leg, being careful not to tear the skin. Salt and pepper the entire bird, including the inside, with 1 tablespoon salt and 3 cranks of pepper.

Rub the bird with 2 tablespoons oil and place in a roasting pan. Bake for 20 minutes.

Baste with another 2 tablespoons oil and reduce the temperature to 325 degrees. Leave the door open for 1 minute and then bake for another 35 to 45 minutes, basting often with pan juices. If the chicken browns too quickly, cover with aluminum foil.

Turn the oven off and let the chicken rest for 10 minutes. During this time, in a large Teflon pan, heat 1 tablespoon of vegetable oil and lightly brown the onion over medium heat. Salt and pepper to taste and add the onion to the juices in the bottom of the roasting pan.

In the Teflon pan, heat remaining oil over high heat and lightly brown the mushroom slices with butter and salt and pepper to taste. After 1 minute in the pan, add the mushrooms to the juices in the bottom of the roasting pan.

Carve the bird by removing both legs and separating at the knee. Remove both breasts and slice into 4 pieces each. Place the meat on a platter and spoon the mushroom and onion jus over the chicken. Garnish with remaining chopped chives.

WINE PAIRING
Mayor de Migueloa Rioja Reserva 1997

FISH

PAN-SEARED CAROLINA GOLDEN TROUT
OVER YOUNG VEGETABLES IN A GRAPEFRUIT BUTTER SAUCE

SERVES 6

VEGETABLES

12 baby carrots, peeled and blanched

12 baby leeks, blanched

1 baby golden beet, peeled and blanched

12 baby purple beets, peeled and blanched

12 baby turnips, peeled and blanched

TROUT

3 large golden trout (1 large fillet per person), de-bone pin bones, score the skin

1 1/2 tablespoons salt

6 to 8 cranks fresh-ground white pepper

6 tablespoons virgin olive oil, divided

SAUCE

3 pink grapefruits, juiced

1 cup Plugra brand unsalted butter, chilled and divided

1/4 cup water

1 1/2 tablespoons salt, divided

6 cranks fresh-ground white pepper, divided

1 pink grapefruit, peeled and cut into segments for garnish

Amaranth sprouts for garnish

1 bunch fresh chives

Preheat oven to 400 degrees.

If you haven't already done so, separately blanch all baby vegetables in salted boiling water. Chill and set aside.

Season the 6 trout fillets with approximately 1 1/2 tablespoons salt and 6 to 8 cranks of pepper.

In a large Teflon pan, heat 3 tablespoons oil and sear the trout skin side down for 1 minute. You want to get the skin crispy so sear just two fillets at a time, skin side only.

Remove the fillets from the pan rare and set on an oiled baking pan, skin side up.

Deglaze the sauté pan with the grapefruit juice and reduce to a syrup consistency or 1/2 cup juice. Slowly whisk 2/3 cup cold butter into the grapefruit juice over low heat. When all the butter has emulsified into the juice, remove from heat and keep warm.

In a medium saucepan, warm all the baby vegetables except the beets in 1/4 cup of butter and 1/4 cup of water. Add 1 tablespoon salt and 4 cranks of pepper.

Heat the purple beets by themselves in another pan with 2 tablespoons of butter, 1/2 tablespoon salt, 2 cranks of pepper and a tablespoon of water.

Bake the trout for 3 to 4 minutes (do not overcook; keep medium-rare to medium).

While the trout is in the oven, arrange 3 of each baby vegetable along the centers of the plates. Remove the trout from the oven and gently place 1 fillet per person over the baby vegetables.

Wander some grapefruit segments and Amaranth sprouts over the fish and spoon 1 1/2 to 2 tablespoons of sauce over each dish. Garnish with chopped fresh chives.

WINE PAIRING

Zilliken Riesling Kabinett, Mosel-Saar-Ruwer 1994

SAUTÉED BARRAMUNDI OVER OXTAIL WHIPPED POTATOES & CHANTERELLES IN A PINOT NOIR BUTTER

OXTAIL
3 tablespoons vegetable oil

2 tablespoons salt

6 cranks fresh-ground white pepper

1 medium oxtail, cut in half

1 large onion, chopped

1 small leek, cleaned and diced

1 large carrot, peeled and diced

2 cloves garlic, chopped

1 bunch fresh thyme

2 stems rosemary

4 cups dry white wine

2 bay leaves

WHIPPED POTATOES
3 large russet potatoes, peeled and cut into 8 pieces

1 tablespoon kosher salt

1/4 cup whole milk

1/2 cup heavy cream

3/4 cup unsalted butter, diced into cubes, chilled and divided

12 ounces braised oxtail meat pulled (see recipe)

2 shallots, chopped fine

1 clove garlic, chopped fine

4 cranks fresh-ground white pepper

16 chanterelle mushrooms, stems scraped clean

1 tablespoon fresh thyme leaves

BARRAMUNDI
3/4 cup unsalted butter, divided

2 teaspoons salt

8 cranks fresh-ground white pepper

4 6-ounce portions skinless barramundi fillet

3 shallots, chopped fine

3 cups Pinot Noir wine

1 cup oxtail bouillon

1 branch thyme

12 poached baby carrots for garnish

Preheat oven to 375 degrees.

To prepare the oxtail, heat oil in a medium-sized pot. Salt and pepper all sides of the oxtail and sear all sides over medium heat. Add the onion, leek, carrot, garlic, thyme and rosemary.

Lightly brown all the vegetables for 5 to 10 minutes. Once browned, add the white wine and bay leaves and cover all ingredients with cold water. Simmer for 3 1/2 to 4 hours over a low heat until you can pull the meat from the bone easily. Remove the meat and chill. Strain the oxtail bouillon and reserve.

To prepare the potatoes, in a stainless pot cover the potatoes with cold water and the salt. Cook for approximately 30 minutes until tender and then drain.

In another small pot, bring the milk and cream to a boil. Push the potatoes through a food mill and fold in the hot milk and cream with a rubber spatula a little at a time. At the same time, add 8 tablespoons cold butter in small pieces and season with salt and white pepper to taste.

In a medium-sized Teflon pan, heat 4 tablespoons butter over medium heat and sear the oxtail meat for 1 minute. Add the shallots and garlic, season with 1 tablespoon salt and 3 cranks of pepper and cook for another minute. Add the chanterelles and cook for another minute (don't brown them) and add the fresh thyme. Fold the oxtail, shallots, mushrooms and thyme mixture into the whipped potatoes. Keep warm and check the seasoning.

To prepare the barramundi, melt 6 tablespoons butter in a large sauté pan over medium-high heat. Salt and pepper all sides of the barramundi fillets and sear all 4 fillets at the same time for 1 minute on each side for a light coloration. Remove the fillets and bake for 4 to 6 minutes until tender and just cooked.

Add the chopped shallots to the sauté pan and cook for 30 seconds over low heat—do not brown. Deglaze the pan with the red wine, 1 cup of the reserved oxtail bouillon and fresh thyme and reduce to 1/4 cup.

Over a low heat, whisk in the remaining butter, and season with salt and fresh-ground white pepper to taste.

Place the whipped potatoes, oxtail and chanterelles in the center of the plate with the seared barramundi over the top. Spoon a small amount of the red wine sauce over the fish and garnish with poached baby carrots.

Who says fish needs to be served with white wine?

WINE PAIRING

St. Innocent Pinot Noir Anden Vineyard, Willamette Valley 2004

JUMBO LUMP BLUE CRAB GALETTE
IN A LIME, PEAR TOMATO & AVOCADO SALSA

CRAB

1 pound jumbo lump crabmeat, cleaned

2 egg whites

2 tablespoons mayonnaise

1 teaspoon Old Bay seasoning

1 teaspoon dry mustard

1 pinch celery seed

1 pinch cayenne pepper

4 ounces kataifi (shredded phyllo dough)

2 tablespoons grapeseed oil (may substitute vegetable oil)

SALSA

6 limes, removed into segments, save the juice

1 tablespoon salt

4 cranks pepper

1 shallot, chopped fine

1 clove garlic, chopped fine

1 tablespoon chopped chives

6 tablespoons virgin olive oil

2 ripe avocados, diced

2 ounces pea shoots

Preheat oven to 350 degrees.

Combine crab, egg whites, mayonnaise and seasonings. Form into cakes and roll lightly in shredded phyllo dough. There are no breadcrumbs, so the mix will be a little loose.

Heat oil in a skillet over medium-high heat. Sear the crab cakes until golden brown on both sides and warm in the center (about 2 minutes each side).

Heat in the oven for 5 minutes.

To create the salsa, squeeze the juice from the leftover segments of the limes. Add the salt, pepper, shallot, garlic, chives, and finish with the oil and avocado pieces.

Spoon even amounts of the salsa over the galettes and garnish with the pea shoots.

WINE PAIRING

J. Prieur Puligny-Montrachet Les Combettes 1er Cru 1997

SPINY LOBSTER BAKED WITH FENNEL BUTTER

2 fennel bulbs and tops

1/2 bottle Chardonnay

1 cup unsalted butter, room
temperature

1 tablespoon salt

4 cranks fresh-ground white
pepper

3 tablespoons fennel tops,
chopped

4 tablespoons pastis (French
anise apéritif), divided

2 large spiny lobsters (2 to 3
pounds each)

SERVES 4

Preheat oven to 375 degrees.

Cut off the fennel tops at the bulb. Split the bulb in half and cut out the hard center core. Place the fennel in a stainless pot and cover with water and the wine. Simmer 15 minutes or until the fennel is completely cooked. Remove the fennel from the pot and purée in a blender or food processor until a smooth purée is made. Chill.

Once chilled, blend the purée with the butter, salt, pepper, fennel tops, and 2 tablespoons pastis in a mixer.

For each lobster, take the largest, dullest knife you have in the kitchen, force the tip of the blade down through the head of the lobster lengthwise. Follow down across the back and through the tail, splitting the lobster in half. Once in half, remove the small pouch at the tip of the inside of the head. This is the stomach. You'll know because there will be a bit of lobster antennae in there. They like to bite each other's antennae; hence, a live lobster with long antennae in a tank hasn't been there long.

Now that you have removed the stomach, there is a dark, thin tube running along the shell side of the tail. Remove this also and the operation has been a success. Pour remaining pastis over ice and 1/2 cup of water and drink . . . you've earned it!

Place the lobster halves shell side down on a large baking sheet and set aside.

Spread the fennel butter evenly across the meat of the 4 halves of lobster tails and bake for 15 minutes. The butter will stay in the tail. Keep applying butter to baste the tails while they are baking.

With kitchen tongs, gently remove the lobster halves and place them on four large dinner plates. Their antennae will hang off the plates. If you have any fennel butter remaining, make one spread across the tails and serve.

A fun way to finish this dish would be to add the Vegetable Pearls recipe (see page 77) to the cavity of the head of the lobster. It will mix with the now cooked roe or as we call it, "goop"!

WINE PAIRING

Giaconda Chardonnay Nantua Les Deux, Victoria 2003

GRILLED ATLANTIC SALMON WITH
YOUNG FENNEL BULBS IN A BLOOD ORANGE SALSA

3 blood oranges, cut into segments

Blood orange juice (left from segments)

2 oranges, cut into segments

1 lemon, juiced

1 shallot, chopped

1 small clove garlic, chopped

1 tablespoon chopped parsley

1 tablespoon salt

3 cranks white pepper

1/2 cup olive oil

24 ounces salmon (skin and bones removed)

4 baby fennel (blanched)

1/2 cup olive oil

2 tablespoons salt

4 cranks fresh-ground white pepper

4 pinches micro parsley for garnish

SERVES 4

Cut the blood oranges into segments by slicing down the inside of the white membrane to the center of the orange. Squeeze the juice of what is left and cook it in a stainless pot down to a syrup stage. Chill the syrup and set aside.

Repeat this process for the regular oranges, saving the juice. Add lemon juice to the regular orange juice. Then add the shallot, garlic, parsley, salt, pepper and 1/2 cup oil and let this mixture sit at room temperature for at least a half hour.

Preheat your outdoor grill.

Toss the salmon and fennel in 1/2 cup oil. Salt and pepper each side of the salmon and fennel using 1/4 teaspoon salt and 1 crank of fresh pepper.

To help keep the fish from sticking, run an old towel dipped in oil across the grill. Place the salmon and half the fennel in a not so blazing area of the grill and let sear 1 minute on each side. Remove them and place them on a metal pie pan. When ready to eat, place the metal pan on the grill and close the grill lid. Let cook for 30 seconds or longer depending on how well done you want the fish.

Add segments of both oranges to the juice mixture and slice in the remaining fennel. Taste and re-season with salt and pepper if necessary. Spoon the sauce over the salmon and fennel, making sure you spoon from the bottom of the bowl to get the full flavors. Garnish each salmon with the micro parsley.

WINE PAIRING

Guigal Condrieu La Doriane, Rhône Valley 2001

DAYBOAT RED SNAPPER FILLET OVER BABY SPINACH, SWEET WADMALAW ONIONS & POTATO PEARLS IN A CINNAMON CAP MUSHROOM JUS

2 large potatoes, peeled and cut into small rounds with a melon baller

2 cups water

4 teaspoons salt, divided

11 cranks fresh-ground white pepper, divided

1 clove garlic, chopped

8 tablespoons butter, divided

24 ounces fresh snapper fillet (6 ounces per person)

3 large onions, cut into 1/2-inch-wide onion rings

10 ounces baby spinach leaves

1/2 pound cinnamon cap mushrooms

1/2 cup reduced chicken stock

2 bunches fresh chives, chopped

SERVES 4

Preheat oven to 325 degrees.

Poach the small potato balls in 2 cups of water with 2 teaspoons salt, 3 cranks of pepper and garlic until tender. Strain and set aside.

In a large sauté pan, heat 1 tablespoon butter and brown the skin side of the snapper for 2 minutes. Turn and brown the other side for another minute. Bake for 7 to 10 minutes, until just cooked.

Add the large onion rings to the snapper pan with 1 tablespoon butter, 1 tablespoon salt and 4 cranks of pepper. Salt and pepper both sides of each fillet with 1/4 teaspoon salt and 1 crank of pepper each side. Cook for 10 to 12 minutes over medium heat without browning, until tender. Add the spinach leaves, potato balls and mushrooms. Cook for 30 seconds. Add the chicken stock and chives.

Remove the snapper from the oven and spoon some onions, potatoes, mushrooms and sauce over each fillet.

WINE PAIRING

Cuvaison Chardonnay, Carneros 2004

CREEK FLOUNDER SAUTÉED IN A DICED SHRIMP, LIME & CAPER BUTTER

8 tablespoons unsalted butter chilled and cut into cubes, divided

2 1/2 teaspoons salt

18 cranks fresh-ground white pepper

10 ounces fresh flounder fillet, bones and skin removed

4 wild American shrimp, diced raw

1 small shallot, chopped fine

1/4 cup dry white wine

1 lemon, skin removed and cut into segments (save the juice)

1 tablespoon capers

1 tablespoon chopped parsley

SERVES 2

In a small Teflon pan, heat 2 tablespoons butter.

Salt and pepper the flounder with 1/4 teaspoon salt and 1 crank pepper on each side and diced shrimp with 1/4 teaspoon salt and 2 cranks pepper on each side. Sear the flounder for 1 minute on each side and remove from the pan.

In the same hot pan, toss in the diced shrimp and sauté for 30 seconds. Remove from the pan.

Add the shallot to the same pan over low heat and cook without browning for 15 seconds. Add the wine and reduce by half over low heat.

To make the sauce, gently whisk in 6 tablespoons cold butter. Add the lemon juice, capers, parsley and diced shrimp.

Place the flounder fillet in the center of a plate and garnish with the lemon segments.

Pepper the sauce and lightly salt it, as the capers will bring salt to the dish. Spoon the sauce over the flounder.

WINE PAIRING

Prá Soave Monte Grande, Veneto 2004

SAUTÉED CAROLINA RIVER PRAWNS WITH AN HERBED CRÈME FRAICHE

1/2 cup crème fraiche

1 lemon, juiced

1 1/3 tablespoons salt

15 cranks fresh-ground pepper

2 tablespoons fresh tarragon leaves

1 tablespoon fresh chives

2 shallots, chopped fine

1 tablespoon pastis (French apéritif)

6 large freshwater prawns, deveined (shells removed from the tails only)

1 tablespoon olive oil for the prawns

In a small bowl, mix the crème fraiche, lemon juice, 1/2 tablespoon salt, 3 cranks of pepper, tarragon, chives, shallots and pastis. Taste for seasoning and then chill.

Heat the grill.

Season the prawns, using 1/8 teaspoon salt (a tiny pinch) and 1 crank of pepper. Toss the prawns in the oil and grill for 1 minute on each side.

Spoon a small amount of the herbed cream sauce over each prawn tail.

You may find the wonderful shrimp raised in ponds in Camden, South Carolina, but you'll probably need to substitute large shrimp for this recipe.

WINE PAIRING

Qupé Bien Nacido Cuvée, Santa Barbara County 2004

FROGMORE STEW

POTATOES
20 fingerling potatoes

1 bottle dry white wine

SEAFOOD STOCK
1 cup olive oil

5 pounds fresh fish bones or heads, preferably saltwater fish

Shrimp heads

Lobster heads

8 shallots, chopped

25 small cloves garlic

3 pounds seeded Roma tomatoes

1 bunch fresh thyme

6 bay leaves

4 tablespoons Old Bay seasoning

1 lemon, sliced into 6 segments

2 bottles dry white wine (Sauvignon Blanc or Chardonnay)

3 bottles amber beer

1 gallon cold water

2 tablespoons tomato paste

3 to 4 tablespoons salt, to taste

5 to 8 cranks fresh-ground white pepper, to taste

GARNISH
6 whole ears of corn with husk

2 1/2 pounds andouille sausage, cut into 1-inch sections

1 tablespoon vegetable oil

30 fresh wild American shrimp, peeled and deveined, leaving tail intact (save heads and shells for the stock)

2 pounds blue crabmeat, shells removed (if you can get live crabs, simmer in the stock above for 5 minutes then remove and set aside)

25 yellow and red pear tomatoes

1 tablespoon salt

1 bunch chives

SERVES 5

Poach the fingerling potatoes. Simmer until tender in a pot with wine. Add enough water to cover the potatoes. Once tender, remove the potatoes and set aside. Save the wine to add to the sauce.

To prepare the stock, add the oil and sear the fish bones or heads, shrimp heads and lobster heads in a large pot and cook over a high heat until they are lightly browned. It's okay if they stick to the bottom; that's more flavor for your stock.

Add the shallots and garlic and cook over medium heat 5 minutes more. Add the tomatoes, thyme, bay leaves, Old Bay seasoning and lemon.

Pour in the wine and the wine from poached fingerling potatoes, and the beer. Add the cold water and tomato paste. Bring to a boil and simmer slowly for 1 1/2 to 2 hours.

While the stock is simmering, grill the corn until the husk is black. Remove the husk and cut the corn kernels from the cob with a sharp knife. Set the kernels aside.

In a large stainless steel pot, sear the sausage in the oil until lightly browned. Remove the sausage pieces and set aside.

In that same oil, quickly sear the shrimp 10 seconds on each side, keeping them medium-rare. Remove the shrimp and set aside.

After the stock you prepared above has simmered 1 1/2 to 2 hours, strain it and season with salt and fresh-ground pepper.

Deglaze the pot with the seafood stock. Simmer for 20 minutes uncovered.

Just before serving, add the corn, crab, pear tomatoes, fingerling potatoes and 3 sausage pieces. At the last second, add the shrimp. Taste and re-season with salt and pepper if necessary.

Serve in large bowls and garnish with chopped chives tips.

TIP: Keep tasting this as you make it because pepper becomes stronger. Salt and pepper to taste.

WINE PAIRING
Trefethen Chardonnay Oak Knoll, Napa Valley 2004

ROASTED SPOT-TAIL BASS OVER GREEN LENTILS BRAISED IN PINOT NOIR

3 ounces smoked bacon, diced

1 onion chopped

4 cloves garlic, chopped

1/2 leek, washed and diced

1 carrot, peeled and diced

9 ounces lentils du puy (French green lentils)

1 quart red wine (Burgundy)

1 quart veal stock (glace)

2 branches thyme

1 branch rosemary

2 bay leaves

1 tablespoon salt

4 cranks fresh-ground white pepper

BASS

1/2 teaspoon salt

2 cranks fresh-ground white pepper

24 ounces fresh, skinless, boneless spot-tail bass (also called redfish)

2 tablespoons unsalted butter

4 pea shoots for garnish

SERVES 4

Preheat oven to 300 degrees.

To prepare the lentils, lightly brown the diced bacon with the onion and garlic for 2 minutes in a good-sized pot. Add the leek and carrot. Cook another 2 minutes.

Add the lentils and cover with the red wine, veal stock, thyme, rosemary and bay leaves. Cover the pot and bake for 45 minutes.

Test the lentils for doneness and add salt and white pepper to taste.

Preheat oven to 375 degrees.

Salt and pepper the fish, using 1/4 teaspoon and 1 crank of pepper for each side.

In a large sauté pan, heat the butter and sear the bass 1 1/2 minutes on each side. Remove the bass from the pan and bake for 4 minutes.

Place the bass over the lentils with a sprout of pea shoots. The lentils act as the vegetable and sauce for this rustic dish.

WINE PAIRING

Marchese Antinori Chianti Classico Riserva 2000

PAN-SEARED TRIGGERFISH

1 gallon water

2 1/2 tablespoons salt, divided

1 lemon, juiced

2 celery root balls

1 cup whipping cream

3 cranks fresh-ground white
pepper

3 cups oil

1 large russet potato, peeled

3 tablespoons butter, divided

6 6-ounce portions triggerfish

7 teaspoons salt, divided

13 cranks fresh-ground white
pepper, divided

4 shallots, sliced fine

1/2 bottle red wine

8 tablespoons butter for
sauce, diced and kept cold

3 tablespoons chopped
flat-leaf parsley

1 pound lump crabmeat,
drained

Micro chives for garnish

SERVES 6

Preheat oven to 400 degrees.

Heat the water in a large pot with 1 tablespoon salt and the lemon juice. With a sharp knife, cut the outside skins of the celery root and cut the clean celery into fourths. Drop the celery into the simmering lemon water and cook over medium heat for approximately 30 minutes or until knife tender.

In a small pot, bring the whipping cream to a boil.

Place the cooked and drained celery root into a blender with 1 1/2 table-spoons salt and 3 cranks of pepper. Add the hot cream. Cover the blender and slowly blend to create a fine purée. Make sure the cream is hot or the purée will become grainy. Re-season if necessary and pour into a stainless steel pot. Cover the pot and keep it warm on the stove.

Heat the 3 cups oil to 350 degrees in a deep pot. Thinly slice the peeled potatoes on a mandolin. You'll want to create very thin potato chips. Lay them on top of each other and cut them into fine slivers. Rinse the slivers several times in cold water to remove the starch, so they won't stick together when fried.

Dry the potato slivers in a towel. Fry them in the hot oil to a light brown and let them dry on a paper towel. Set aside.

Heat 1 1/2 tablespoons butter in a medium-sized pan over medium to high heat. Season each side of the triggerfish with 1/2 teaspoon salt and 1 crank of pepper. Place 3 of the fillets in the hot pan and sear 1 1/2 minutes on each side to lightly brown. Repeat for the remaining fillets with the remaining 1 1/2 tablespoons butter.

Set all seared fillets on a baking sheet and set aside.

Add the sliced shallots to the pan used to brown the triggerfish and cook over low heat until lightly browned. Add the 1/2 bottle wine and reduce to 1/4 cup liquid with the shallots. Drop to low heat and whisk in the cubes of cold diced butter, a little at a time.

Add 1 teaspoon salt and 3 cranks of pepper. Add the chopped parsley.

Place the triggerfish baking sheet in the oven for 3 minutes. Remove from the oven. Add the crabmeat to the celery purée and re-season with salt and pepper, if necessary. Put some crab-celery on each plate. Place the triggerfish on top. Spoon some sauce around. Garnish with the thin fried potatoes and micro chives.

WINE PAIRING

Mayor de Migueloa Rioja Reserva 1997

GRILLED SPANISH MACKEREL WITH YELLOW TOMATOES & YOUNG OKRA IN AN OPAL BASIL VINAIGRETTE

SERVES 2

SAUCE

6 medium-sized shrimp, peeled and deveined

1 teaspoon salt

3 cranks fresh-ground white pepper

2 tablespoons olive oil

4 limes, cut into segments (save the juice)

1 teaspoon salt

3 cranks fresh-ground white pepper

1 tablespoon chopped shallots

1 teaspoon chopped garlic

20 niçoise olives, pitted and sliced

10 opal basil leaves, stems removed and rough chopped

1/4 cup fine olive oil

FILLETS

2 7-ounce fresh mackerel fillets, skinned and pin bones removed

1 1/2 teaspoons salt, divided

6 cranks fresh-ground white pepper, divided

1 large yellow tomato, peeled and sliced into quartered slices

3 tablespoons grapeseed oil for grilling

8 baby green okra

Light your grill.

To prepare the shrimp, salt and pepper them and toss them in 2 tablespoons olive oil. Grill to medium-rare, 30 seconds each side. Dice into large pieces. Place in a bowl.

Save the juice from the limes and pour over the shrimp. Add 1 teaspoon salt and 3 cranks pepper. Add the shallots, garlic, olives, basil, lime segments and olive oil. Set aside.

Season each mackerel fillet with 1/4 teaspoon salt and 1 crank pepper on each side. Salt and pepper the 4 tomato slices with 1/4 teaspoon salt and 1 crank pepper on each side.

Dip each fillet and tomato slice in the grapeseed oil and set aside. Toss the okra in the remaining oil and grill for about 2 minutes, turning often to leave light grill marks.

On the hot side of the grill, grill each tomato slice 30 seconds on one side only. Then cook the mackerel fillets 20 seconds each side.

Stack the okra, tomatoes and mackerel fillets onto serving plates. Spoon some sauce over the top.

WINE PAIRING

Zind-Humbrecht Gewürztraminer Hengst, Grand Cru, Alsace 2001

BLACK GROUPER WITH DIVER SCALLOP MOUSSE, BAKED IN SWISS CHARD IN A CAPER, SUN-DRIED TOMATO, PICHOLINI OLIVE BUTTER

MOUSSE

3/4 pounds dry-pack scallops

1 tablespoon kosher salt

4 cranks fresh-ground white pepper

1 cup heavy cream

8 large leaves Swiss chard, stems out and blanched

2 tablespoons olive oil (to paint "pucks")

BLACK GROUPER

2 tablespoons olive oil

1 teaspoon salt

4 cranks fresh-ground white pepper

24 ounces black grouper, skin and bones removed (4 6-ounce fillets)

SAUCE

2 shallots, chopped fine

2 cups Chardonnay

1/2 cup unsalted butter, cubed and chilled

2 tablespoons sun-dried tomatoes, diced fine

1 tablespoon capers

1 tablespoon fresh thyme leaves

4 cranks pepper

2 tablespoons picholini olives, pitted and sliced

16 sea cress sprouts for garnish

SERVES 4

Preheat oven to 375 degrees.

Place your food processor container, top and blade in the freezer 1 hour prior to starting this recipe. When making any mousse, the cooler the processor, the better for all raw ingredients.

Remove your food processor container, top and blade from the freezer. Drop in scallops, salt and pepper and pulse to purée. Once almost completely puréed, add in a stream of cream until blended. Do not over blend or you will heat up the mousse.

Lay the blanched swiss chard leaves out flat on a clean table surface, laying 2 leaves per person, overlapping slightly. Place 1/4 of the mousse in the center of the leaves and pull the leaves in and over the top of the mousse to hide it. This will be the bottom, so now turn over each of the mousse "pucks" and refrigerate on a baking sheet.

To cook the grouper, heat the olive oil in a large sauté pan. Salt and pepper each side of the grouper fillets with 1/4 teaspoon salt and 1 crank of pepper for each side. Sear them in the oil over medium-high heat for 30 seconds on each side to lightly brown. Remove the fillets and place them on the baking sheet with the pucks.

In the same sauté pan, add the shallots and drop heat to low. Cook 30 seconds. Add the Chardonnay and reduce to 1/2 cup liquid. Drop the flame to very low and very slowly whisk in the cold butter, sun-dried tomatoes, capers, thyme, pepper and olives. Keep this on the burner at a warm temperature. Do not re-boil this sauce or let it cool down; either will cause it to break.

With 2 tablespoons olive oil, paint the scallop pucks and bake with the grouper fillets for 5 minutes. Place each puck in the center of four bowls. Place 1 grouper fillet over each mousse puck. Stir the sauce, taste and re-season if necessary. Spoon the sauce over each fillet and garnish with sea cress sprouts.

WINE PAIRING

Grosset Riesling Polish Hill, Clare Valley 2005

OKEECHOBEE CATFISH IN CRAYFISH SAUCE

CRAYFISH BOUILLON

30 whole live crayfish

1 tablespoon vegetable oil

1/2 leek, split, rinsed and sliced

1/2 carrot, peeled and sliced into rounds

1/2 bottle dry white wine

1/2 gallon water

4 thyme branches

1 bay leaf

10 white peppercorns

1/2 tablespoon salt

CATFISH

2 7-ounce fillets of catfish, skin removed

2 1/2 teaspoons salt, divided

9 cranks fresh-ground white pepper, divided

1 1/2 tablespoons butter, divided

2 shallots, chopped fine

6 ounces homemade andouille sausage

1 tablespoon cognac

1 cup Crayfish Bouillon (see recipe)

1 1/2 cups whipping cream

1 tablespoon fresh-chopped basil

10 red pear tomatoes, cut in half

10 yellow pear tomatoes, cut in half

1 teaspoon olive oil

SERVES 2

To make the bouillon, place the live crayfish in a large pot and run warm water over them for 20 to 30 minutes to purge and rinse them. While they're doing their thing, prepare their bath with a medium-sized pot.

Heat the oil and add the leek and carrot, lightly browning them. Deglaze with the wine and add the water, thyme, bay leaf, peppercorns and salt. Simmer for 30 minutes while the crayfish are purging.

Bring the crayfish bouillon to a boil and toss all the crayfish in, if there is room. If not, do this twice.

Let the crayfish simmer for 3 minutes, then strain the entire pot. Save the bouillon, don't pour it down the drain—voice of experience here!

Run cold water over the crayfish to chill them. Set two whole crayfish aside for garnish. Pull the tails from the heads and set aside. Peel the tail shell from the tails. Set the tails aside.

Season each side of the catfish with 1/4 teaspoon salt and 1 crank pepper. Heat 1 tablespoon butter in a medium-sized pan over medium heat and sear the fillets 1 minute on each side. Remove from the pan.

Add the shallots to the pan with 1/2 tablespoon butter and brown the sausage. Remove the sausage, leaving the shallots. Deglaze the pan with the cognac and bouillon. Bring to a boil. Add the cream and the 30 crayfish heads. Add 1/2 tablespoon salt and 3 cranks of pepper.

Simmer this sauce slowly to extract as much flavor from the heads as possible. If possible, crush the heads while simmering in the sauce.

After 10 minutes, strain the sauce and reduce to a sauce consistency. Add the sausage and basil to this sauce.

Sear the tomatoes in olive oil for 20 seconds with 1/2 teaspoon salt and 2 cranks pepper. Add the seared fillets to the sauce. Add the crayfish tails and the pear tomatoes.

Heat 1 minute over medium heat to bring up temperature; do not boil. Place the catfish fillets in the center of each plate and spoon some of the sauce over top. Garnish with one whole crayfish. Bon appetite!

WINE PAIRING

Schmitts Kinder Sylvaner Spätlese Trocken, Franken 2003

Desserts

"A LA MINUTE" THIN APPLE TART WITH HONEY ICE CREAM

HONEY ICE CREAM

2 cups milk

2 cups heavy cream

6 egg yolks

1 cup sugar

1/2 cup honey

TART

2 sheets frozen prepared
  puff pastry

4 Granny Smith apples

Sugar for sprinkling

4 tablespoons butter

SERVES 4

Preheat oven to 375 degrees.

To prepare the ice cream, heat the milk and cream to a boil.

Combine yolks and sugar in a medium bowl. Whisk hot milk mixture into eggs, little by little. Whisk in honey and let cool. Freeze in an ice cream machine according to the manufacturer's directions.

Slightly thaw the puff pastry sheets. Cut out four 6-inch circles and place on a non-greased, non-lined pan.

Peel, core and thinly slice the apples and arrange in a circular fan over the puff pastry. Sprinkle with sugar.

Cube all of the butter and sprinkle on the apples. Bake for approximately 20 minutes or until golden brown.

Remove the tart from the oven and place on individual plates. Spoon a large spoonful of Honey Ice Cream over the top. I know you're wanting to add cinnamon to this. Please don't! You can actually eat apple pies without cinnamon.

WINE PAIRING

Tenuta S. Anna Picolit, Friuli 1999

THE TRUE CRÈME BRULÉE

12 egg yolks

2 cups sugar

1 pint milk

1 vanilla bean, scraped

1 1/2 quarts heavy cream

1/2 cup brown sugar

1/2 cup white sugar

Ripe berries for garnish

SERVES 6

Preheat oven to 300 degrees.

In a large bowl, combine yolks and sugar and whisk until combined and smooth.

In a medium-sized saucepan, combine the milk and vanilla bean scrapings. Heat to a boil. Remove the pot from the heat and let cool for 10 minutes. In a large bowl, slowly whisk the warm milk into the egg and sugar mixture. Then whisk the cream into the yolks.

Pour the brûlée mix into six cups, filling to 1/2 inch from the rim of the cup.

When you have filled all six cups, place them in a pan half-filled with water and cover with aluminum foil.

Bake the brûlées for 1 hour or until set. Let cool to room temperature and refrigerate before serving.

With a small sifter, sprinkle a mixture of the brown and white sugars together. Shake over the tops of the dishes to form a thin layer of sugar.

Take a small rag and wipe along the edges to remove sugar from the rim of the bowls, without touching the brûlée mix. Get a small torch and carefully burn the sugar on top of the brûlées, starting from 2 to 3 inches away, to slowly melt the sugar together.

Top with fresh berries or ripe fruits and serve quickly because the hard caramel (brûlée) will start breaking up after 3 to 4 minutes.

WINE PAIRING

Yalumba Muscat "Museum Reserve," South Australia

THIN CRÊPES STUFFED WITH PRALINE GRITS & PISTACHIO ICE CREAM

PRALINE GRITS

2 1/4 cups milk

2 1/2 tablespoons
  unsalted butter

1/2 cup stone-ground grits

1 to 2 cups heavy cream,
  divided

1/2 cup praline paste
  (sweet hazelnut purée)

CRÊPES

2 cups flour

1 teaspoon sugar

1 pinch salt

2 eggs, beaten

2 1/2 cups milk

1 tablespoon melted butter

PISTACHIO ICE CREAM

5 egg yolks

1/2 cup sugar

2 1/4 cups whole milk

1 1/2 tablespoons
  pistachio paste

1/2 cup green pistachios

DRIZZLE

1/4 cup fine dark chocolate

SERVES 8

To prepare the grits, bring the milk and butter to a boil in a thick-bottomed saucepan. Stir in the grits and return to a boil. Reduce heat, allowing the grits to cook for another 15 minutes at a low boil until the grits are thick and have absorbed most of the milk. Stir occasionally to keep the grits from sticking.

Add 1/2 cup of the heavy cream to the pot and reduce the heat, allowing the grits to cook slowly for another 10 minutes. As the liquid is absorbed, add more cream. After cooking at least an hour, the grits should be thick and full bodied. Fold in the praline paste just before serving and stir well. Do not re-heat, as praline paste is mostly oil and will break easily.

To prepare the crêpes, sift the flour, sugar and salt into a bowl and make a well in the center. Mix the eggs and milk. Slowly pour this mixture into the well, whisking all the time to incorporate the flour mixture until you have a smooth batter. Add the melted butter and cover. Let rest for at least 1 hour.

Heat a crêpe pan or non-stick saucepan and grease it with a small amount of melted butter. Pour in enough batter to barely cover the bottom of the pan and quickly lean the pan sideways to spread the batter as thin as you can across the bottom of the pan. Cook for 30 seconds or until lightly brown. Flip the crêpe and cook an additional 30 seconds on the other side.

To prepare the ice cream, whisk the yolks and sugar together until light, almost fluffy. Heat the milk in a saucepan and bring just to a boil. Pour the hot milk gently over the sugar/yolk mixture, whisking continuously.

Pour the entire mix back into the saucepan and cook over medium low heat, using a large rubber spatula to scrape the bottom as you go. Stir back and forth until thick enough to coat the back of the spatula. Do not let this mix boil or it will separate.

Add the pistachio paste and chill over a bowl of ice to drop the temperature as quickly as possible. Once cool, add the chopped pistachios. Churn in an ice cream maker until it just pulls together, then freeze in an airtight container.

Pull the ice cream from the freezer 20 minutes prior to serving, as it is best when it is just about to melt.

To prepare the drizzle, heat the chocolate in 10 second intervals in the microwave until it is melted. Do not overheat.

To serve, place 1 tablespoon of Praline Grits in the center of a crêpe and pull all of the outer crepe over the grits to form a small pouch. Flip the pouch over and heat in a microwave for 10 seconds. Remove and set the crêpe in the center of a plate. Add a scoop of the ice cream, drizzle with chocolate, and enjoy.

WINE PAIRING

Chapoutier Banyuls 2003

SPICED BERRY MARTINI IN A PINOT NOIR SYRUP
WITH STAR ANISE ICE CREAM

SPICED BERRY MARTINI

1 gallon red wine

5 cups sugar

8 slices oranges, whole

4 slices lemon, whole

30 white peppercorns

8 whole cloves

3 vanilla beans

4 sticks cinnamon

Blueberries, raspberries
  and blackberries

ICE CREAM

2 cups whole milk

10 whole star anise

10 egg yolks

2 cups sugar

2 cups heavy cream

SERVES 8

To make the martini, place all ingredients except berries together in a stock-pot. Cook and reduce down to a syrup stage. Strain and cool. Keep refrigerated until ready to use.

To prepare the ice cream, bring milk and the star anise to a boil in a small saucepan on high heat. Reduce heat and simmer for 5 minutes.

Combine yolks and sugar in a medium bowl. Temper the hot milk into the yolks and pour yolks into the saucepan. Whisk constantly over medium heat until the mixture coats the back of a spoon. Remove from heat and place the pan in an ice bath.

Let cool to room temperature. Strain and discard star anise. Add heavy cream to mixture and whisk to combine.

Freeze in an ice cream machine according to manufacturer's instructions.

Place 1 cup of mixed berries in a serving dish. Pour 1/4 cup of syrup over all. Top with the ice cream.

WINE PAIRING

Quady Elysium, California 2002

SAUTÉED PEACHES & ROASTED PISTACHIOS IN A CHARDONNAY VANILLA SYRUP WITH VANILLA ICE CREAM

VANILLA ICE CREAM

4 vanilla beans,
  split and scraped

2 cups whole milk

10 egg yolks

2 cups sugar

2 cups heavy cream

CHARDONNAY VANILLA SYRUP

1 cup water

1 cup sugar

1 cup Chardonnay

1 vanilla bean, split and
  scraped with a knife

PEACHES

2 tablespoons butter

4 peaches, peeled, pit
  seeds removed and cut
  into quarters

4 tablespoons pistachios

SERVES 4

To prepare the ice cream, add the vanilla beans and scrapings to the milk. Bring milk to a boil in a small saucepan on high heat. Reduce heat and simmer for 5 minutes.

Combine yolks and sugar in a medium bowl. Temper the hot milk into the yolks and pour yolks into the saucepan. Whisk constantly over medium heat until the mixture coats the back of a spoon. Remove from heat and place the pan in an ice bath. Let cool to room temperature. Add heavy cream to mixture and whisk to combine. Remove the vanilla beans. Freeze in an ice cream machine according to manufacturer's instructions.

To prepare the syrup, mix the water, sugar, wine and vanilla bean in a small pot. Bring to a boil and simmer for 15 minutes. Re-scrape the bean into the syrup. Chill.

To make the peaches, in a large sauté pan, heat the butter. When almost brown, add the peaches and sear on high heat, turning as they brown.

Drop the temperature once the peaches are browned, add the vanilla syrup to the hot pan. Bring to a boil and remove from the heat. Add the pistachios.

Spoon four peach pieces per person into bowls, making sure to include pistachios and syrup. Top with the ice cream and serve.

WINE PAIRING

Lilly Pilly Noble Blend, Riverina 2004

KEY LIME CURD WITH RASPBERRIES & TUILLES COOKIES

KEY LIME CURD

3 large egg yolks

2/3 cup sugar

1/3 cup fresh lime juice

4 1/2 tablespoons unsalted butter, cubed and chilled

3/4 tablespoon lime zest

TUILLES COOKIES

10 tablespoons unsalted butter, at room temperature

2/3 cup white sugar

2/3 cup brown sugar

2/3 cup orange juice, warm at room temperature

3/8 cup sifted flour

12 raspberries

SERVES 12

Preheat oven to 350 degrees.

To make the key lime curd, whisk together egg yolks and sugar in a medium-sized stainless bowl until blended well. Add the lime juice and cook over a pot of simmering water, stirring constantly, until the curd thickens, approximately 8 to 10 minutes. Remove from heat and whisk in the cubed butter and lime zest. Cool quickly and wrap with plastic wrap.

To make the Tuilles Cookies, whip butter lightly with the sugars in a mixer. Add the orange juice and slowly add the flour.

On a Teflon baking sheet, drop 1/2 teaspoon drops of cookie mix and bake for 7 to 24 minutes, watching carefully as they brown. The mix will spread out and lightly brown. Resist your urge to touch them to see if they are ready!

Remove the cookies from the oven and let cool. Once cooled, remove the cookies from the pan with a spatula and break into small pieces if needed.

Place a small amount of lime curd on each spoon with a raspberry and a piece of tuilles cookie. Remember, this will go in your mouth all in one shot, so less is more!

This is something fun in a spoon before you bring dessert to the table.

WINE PAIRING

Mount Horrocks Riesling Cordon Cut, Clare Valley 2003

WHOLE ROASTED FIGS
& WILDFLOWER HONEY ICE CREAM

SERVES 6

WILDFLOWER HONEY ICE CREAM

5 egg yolks

1/2 cup sugar

2 1/4 cups whole milk

3 tablespoons wildflower honey

ROASTED FIGS

6 large whole ripe figs

3 teaspoons unsalted butter, divided

6 teaspoons wildflower honey

Wildflower petals for garnish

Preheat oven to 400 degrees.

To prepare the ice cream, whisk the yolks and sugar together until light, almost fluffy.

Heat the milk in a saucepan and bring just to boil. Pour the milk gently over the egg yolk and sugar mixture, whisking continuously. Pour entire mix back into the saucepan and cook over medium-low, using a large rubber spatula to scrape the bottom as you go. Stir back and forth until thick enough to coat the back of the spatula. Do not let this mix boil or it will separate.

Add the honey and chill over a bowl of ice to drop the temperature as quickly as possible. Churn in an ice cream maker until it just pulls together, then freeze in an airtight container. Pull the ice cream out of the freezer 20 minutes prior to serving, as it is best when it is just about to melt.

To prepare the figs, remove the stem of the figs with a sharp knife. Slice down across the top of the fig about half way. Stop and turn the fig. Cut again, making a cross. Stop at the halfway point again.

Open the cross on top of the fig and insert 1/2 teaspoon of butter in each fig. Spoon 1 teaspoon of honey over each fig and bake for 3 to 5 minutes (depending on the ripeness of the figs). Remove the figs from the oven and open the top enough to insert a spoon of ice cream. Garnish with wildflower petals. Serve quickly.

WINE PAIRING

Château d'Yquem, Sauternes 1983

ICE WINE SABAYON & GRILLED PEACHES

4 peaches

2 tablespoons vegetable oil

4 egg yolks

2 tablespoons sugar

1 cup ice wine

SERVES 4

Preheat oven broiler. Light your grill.

Peel each peach, cut in quarters and remove the pits. Toss the peaches in oil and grill 1 1/2 minutes each side on an outdoor grill. Set aside in individual baking dishes.

Fill half of a small pot with water and bring to a boil. You'll use this as a double boiler. Drop the heat so the water gently simmers.

In a medium-sized bowl that will fit on your small pot, whisk the egg yolks, sugar and ice wine together. Place the bowl over the simmering pot.

Over a medium-high heat, whisk the egg yolks, sugar and ice wine continuously for 2 to 3 minutes until the mix thickens. The sugar will cook and the egg yolks will thicken. Do not over-heat or you'll have sweet scrambled eggs. Slow and easy is better, so no phone calls or soap operas while whisking. A quick sip of wine would work!

Pour this thick, sweet sabayon over the grilled peaches and place under the broiler to lightly brown. Keep the oven door open to ensure browning, not burning . . . the difference is only about 4 seconds.

I enjoy the look of browning for this dish, but it's really all about the flavor, not the color.

WINE PAIRING

Inniskillin Vidal Icewine, Niagara Peninsula 2003

PURVEYORS LIST

Anson Mills
803.467.4122
www.ansonmills.com
Grits, cornmeal for hoe cake

Artisan Specialty Food
800.280.3646
Escargot, red wine vinegar, truffle oil, bresaola, sherry vinegar, niçoise

Ashley Farms
336.766.9900
www.ashleyfarms.com
French breed chicken

Broken Arrow Ranch
800.962.4263
www.brokenarrowranch.com
Venison tenderloin

Bliss Maple Syrup
616.942.7545
3759 Broadmoore SE #D
Grand Rapids, MI 49512
Maple syrup

Chef's Garden
800.289.4644
www.chefsgarden.com
Swiss chard, currant tomatoes, baby leeks, beets (golden, baby red), carrots (baby), baby fennel, blood oranges, tomatoes (currant, yellow, pear), baby okra, opal basil, bachelors button, frisée, zucchini blossoms, micro beet sprouts, kumquats, golden beets, micro chives, micro parsley, pea shoots (golden, green), pearl vegetables, sunchokes, haricots verts, salsafy, asparagus (white, green), red ribbon sorrel, baby salad greens, endive, baby arugula, champagne grapes, sunflower sprouts, lola rosa salad, baby cuc-a-melons, purple cauliflower, seacrest, fingerling potatoes, amaranth

Inland Seafood
800.883.3474
www.inlandseafood.com
Salmon (smoked), tuna, scallops, lobster, soft-shell crabs, oysters, wild American shrimp, golden trout, triggerfish, crawfish,

Millissime, LTD
212.366.4863
www.millissime.com
Pecan oil, pistachio oil, walnut oil

Mikuni Wild Harvest
866.993.9927
www.mikuniwildharvest.com
Baby chanterelles, huckleberries, portobella mushrooms, truffles (fresh, summer), shiitake, elf mushrooms, black trumpets, fresh cèpes, cinnamon caps

Pasture to Plate
708.652.3663
www.pasture2plate.com
Foie gras, veal sweetbreads, smoked bacon, bliss bourbon maple syrup, pig's feet, smoked ham hock, smoked chicken, duck breast, wild turkey, Parma prosciutto, quail, pheasant, squab, kurabuta pork, oxtail

Split Creek Farms Dairy
864.287.3921
www.splitcreek.com
Fresh goat cheese

Triar Seafood
800.741.3474
www.triarseafood.com
Okeechobee catfish, halibut, scallops, black grouper, mackerel, skate wing, triggerfish, wild American shrimp, stone crab claws, barramundi, lump crabmeat, spiny lobster, red snapper, flounder, river prawn

Metric Conversion Chart

Liquid and Dry Measures

U.S.	Canadian	Australian
$1/4$ teaspoon	1 mL	1 ml
$1/2$ teaspoon	2 mL	2 ml
1 teaspoon	5 mL	5 ml
1 Tablespoon	15 mL	20 ml
$1/4$ cup	50 mL	60 ml
$1/3$ cup	75 mL	80 ml
$1/2$ cup	125 mL	125 ml
$2/3$ cup	150 mL	170 ml
$3/4$ cup	175 mL	190 ml
1 cup	250 mL	250 ml
1 quart	1 liter	1 litre

Temperature Conversion Chart

Fahrenheit	Celsius
250	120
275	140
300	150
325	160
350	180
375	190
400	200
425	220
450	230
475	240
500	260